500 IDEAS FOR SMALL SPACES
500 IDÉES POUR PETITS ESPACES
500 IDEEN FÜR KLEINE RÄUME

Editorial coordination, editor:
Simone Schleifer

Text:
Daniela Santos Quartino

English translation:
Matthew Clarke

French translation:
Marion Westerhoff

German translation:
Susanne Engler

Proofreading:
Heather Bagott, Marie-Pierre Santamaria, Martin Rolshoven

Art director:
Mireia Casanovas Soley

Graphic design and layout:
Oriol Serra Juncosa

Printed in Spain

ISBN 978-3-8228-2793-2

500 IDEAS FOR SMALL SPACES
500 IDÉES POUR PETITS ESPACES
500 IDEEN FÜR KLEINE RÄUME

EVERGREEN

Contents Sommaire Inhalt

Small homes are increasingly becoming the only option available to many people, on account of high property prices and the need to live in large cities. This trend has not escaped the attention of architecture firms and interior design magazines.

The big issue today is how to take the maximum advantage of space. Consequently, the layout of the various settings in a home and the choice of materials and furniture are crucial when it comes to taking full benefit of the limited space available without giving up comfort. This is the principal challenge, as a living space should not have to sacrifice comfort.

The solutions to this problem often require bold ideas inspired by commercial design and now effectively transplanted to a domestic setting. On other occasions, when the possibilities of altering the form of a home are limited, it is necessary to draw on a wide range of tactics derived from the art of decoration.

The 500 ideas contained in this book are grouped into themes linked to these strategies. The first chapters refer to different types of coverings and the way of applying them to a home to obtain a sense of spaciousness. This is the domain of natural and synthetic textures, along with materials capable of reflecting or absorbing light that can be used on floors, walls and ceilings. The book's focus then turns to the transformative power of lighting and colors, as well as their effect on dimensions and even states of mind.

It is not merely a question of creating visual effects, however. There are real possibilities of extending floor space without pushing back the boundaries of a home, and these are explored in a chapter devoted to different ways of uniting and dividing spaces. Similarly, the equipment placed inside a home can help make it look noticeably bigger. So, in the final chapter, a detailed examination of each room reveals more ideas for maximizing the benefits of furniture and technology in order to make a home the refuge and source of pleasure that we all desire.

De nos jours, nombreux sont ceux qui privilégient essentiellement les petites habitations. Due au prix du mètre carré ou soit à la nécessité de vivre en zone urbaine, cette tendance, qui s'affirme, a le vent en poupe dans les cabinets d'architecture et fait la une des revues de décoration.

Aujourd'hui, la grande question est de savoir comment optimiser l'espace. Dans cette optique, l'aménagement des différentes pièces de la maison, les matériaux et le mobilier s'inscrivent en paramètres clés pour tirer parti des quelques mètres carrés disponibles, sans toutefois renoncer au confort. Et c'est bien là tout le défi, car un espace de vie ne peut se passer de confort.

Très souvent, les solutions s'inspirent d'idées audacieuses appliquées dans les espaces commerciaux et transposées ensuite sur l'habitat individuel. Mais là où les possibilités d'intervention architecturale sur la forme touchent à leurs limites, un large éventail d'idées issues de l'art de la décoration prend la relève.

Les 500 idées contenues dans cet ouvrage sont regroupées par thèmes en fonction des diverses solutions étudiées. Les premiers chapitres exposent des types de revêtement et leurs méthodes d'application pour un agrandissement visuel de la maison. C'est là où entrent en jeu les textures naturelles ou synthétiques, la faculté d'absorption ou de réflexion de la lumière des matériaux utilisés pour les sols, murs et plafonds. Intervient ensuite le pouvoir modificateur de l'éclairage et des couleurs, leur impact sur les dimensions, sans oublier leurs effets sur l'état d'âme des occupants.

Ceci étant, il ne s'agit pas uniquement de créer des effets visuels. A vrai dire, il existe bien des façons d'élargir l'espace sans pour autant agrandir le périmètre de la maison. Un autre chapitre présente les diverses méthodes permettant d'unifier ou diviser l'espace de vie. Idem pour l'équipement de la maison qui contribue tout autant à augmenter visiblement les mètres carrés d'une habitation. Pour cela, au fil d'un parcours minutieux de chaque pièce, un dernier chapitre nous fait découvrir d'autres idées d'optimisation du mobilier, de la technologie et de leurs atouts, pour faire de la maison ce havre de paix et cette source de plaisir tant désirés.

Kleine Wohnungen sind für viele Menschen heutzutage die einzige Wohnmöglichkeit. Das kann an dem hohen Quadratmeterpreis liegen oder an der Tatsache, dass man in einer Großstadt leben muss oder will. Die Tendenz ist steigend und es gibt immer mehr kleine Wohnungen, wie Studien über Architektur und die Zeitschriften für Dekoration und Raumgestaltung beweisen.

Deshalb stellt sich heute die große Frage, wie man den zur Verfügung stehenden Raum maximal nutzen kann. Unter dieser Voraussetzung sind die Aufteilung der Wohnbereiche, die Möbel und das Material Schlüsselelemente, um die wenigen zur Verfügung stehenden Quadratmeter so gut wie möglich zu nutzen, ohne an Bequemlichkeit einzubüßen. Dies ist heutzutage eine große Herausforderung. In einer Wohnung sollte man nicht auf Komfort verzichten müssen.

Deshalb sind oft gewagte Lösungen notwendig, die von Geschäftsräumen inspiriert sind und auf Wohnungen übertragen werden. In manchen Fällen können kaum Eingriffe an der Form und Struktur der Wohnung vorgenommen werden, so dass man Taktiken aus der Raumgestaltung und Dekoration anwenden muss.

Die 500 Ideen, die in diesem Buch enthalten sind, zeigen mögliche Lösungen nach Themen geordnet auf. Die ersten Kapitel beziehen sich auf Verkleidungsmaterialien, und wie man diese einsetzen kann, damit die Wohnung visuell größer wirkt. Dabei geht es um natürliche oder synthetische Materialien, die für Böden, Wände und Decken benutzt werden, und deren Fähigkeit, Licht zu absorbieren oder widerzuspiegeln. Danach wird gezeigt, wie sehr man mit Beleuchtung und Farben einen Raum gestalten kann, und wie sich diese Faktoren auf den visuellen Eindruck, das Empfinden der Größe und das Wohlbefinden auswirken können.

Aber es geht dabei nicht allein um visuelle Effekte. Es gibt auch Möglichkeiten, den Raum zu erweitern, ohne den Umfang des Hauses zu vergrößern. Diese Möglichkeiten werden in dem Kapitel aufgezeigt, indem verschiedene Methoden, den Raum zu teilen oder zu vereinen, dargestellt werden. Ebenso trägt die Ausstattung der Wohnung spürbar dazu bei, den verfügbaren Platz besser zu nutzen. Deshalb werden im letzten Teil alle Räume detailliert beschrieben und viele Ideen gezeigt, wie man Möbel und Technologie einsetzen kann, um aus einer Wohnung ein wahres Heim, einen Ort der Ruhe und des Wohlfühlens zu machen.

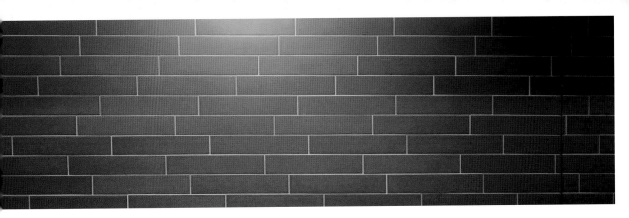

500 IDEAS FOR SMALL SPACES
500 IDÉES POUR PETITS ESPACES
500 IDEEN FÜR KLEINE RÄUME

Wall coverings and ceilings
Revêtements, plafonds et murs
Verkleidungen, Decken und Wände

Smooth, shiny textures help to create bright spacious settings, in conjunction with pale, unbroken colors. Small homes do not necessarily mean either monotony or excessive minimalism. The key is to take advantage of the benefits of the various types of available coverings and imaginatively combine materials and colors to create settings with personality and style.

Les textures lisses et brillantes, ainsi que les couleurs claires et intenses, aident à créer des ambiances diaphanes et spacieuses. Une petite maison n'est pas forcément synonyme de monotonie et minimalisme extrême. Le tout est de savoir tirer parti des avantages qu'offrent les différents types de revêtement et de savoir combiner astucieusement matériaux et couleurs pour créer des univers personnels et stylés.

Glatte, glänzende Texturen und helle, volle Farben lassen transparent wirkende und weite Wohnumgebungen entstehen. Kleine Häuser müssen nicht unbedingt monoton oder übertrieben minimalistisch sein. Wichtig ist es, die Vorteile zu nutzen, die verschiedene Verkleidungsmaterialien bieten, und durch eine geschickte Kombination von Material und Farbton eine persönliche und stilvolle Atmosphäre zu schaffen.

© Gogortza & Llorella

001 Pure white on all the walls provides a modern look, as long as the furniture also includes natural or neutral colors. Fabrics can be used to add splashes of color.

Pour un look contemporain, privilégier le blanc comme couleur unique sur tous les murs, à condition de le combiner avec un mobilier aux tons crus ou neutres. La touche de couleur s'affiche sur les tissus.

Um eine Wohnumgebung modern zu gestalten, eignet sich Weiß ausgezeichnet als einzige Wandfarbe, aber nur dann, wenn die Möbel auch Naturtöne oder neutrale Farben haben. Für etwas Farbigkeit sorgen die Textilien.

002 The application of color to just one or two walls in a room brings a sense of spaciousness.

Appliquer une couleur sur un ou deux murs d'une pièce, pour qu'elle paraisse plus spacieuse.

Wenn man eine oder zwei Wände eines Raums farbig streicht, entsteht der Eindruck von Weite.

003 Matt paint provides the ideal way to give a smooth appearance to walls with imperfections or rustic finishes.

La peinture mate est idéale pour donner un aspect lisse à des murs dotés d'imperfections ou au fini rustique.

Matte Farben eignen sich ausgezeichnet für glatte Wände, die leichte Unebenheiten haben oder rustikal wirken.

© Margherita Spiluttini

© David Frutos/Adhoc MSL

04 Effects created by sponging, streaking or scraping paint are no longer in fashion.
Eviter les finitions de peinture aux effets estompés, veinés ou raclés qui ne sont plus au goût du jour.
Anstriche mit Wischtechnik, Maserieren oder Kammtechnik usw. sind nicht mehr modern.

05 Vibrant colors like orange and green are ideally suited to the back of a plasterboard built-in bookcase.
Les couleurs acidulées comme l'orange et le vert sont idéales pour habiller l'intérieur d'une étagère maçonnée dans le mur.
Kräftige Farben wie Orange und Grün eignen sich ideal für das Innere eines Wandregals aus Pladur.

06 Metallic gray is a newly popular neutral color that goes well with all other colors when applied to either walls or ceilings.
Le gris métallisé, tant sur les murs que sur les plafonds, est la teinte neutre en vogue car elle se marie bien avec toutes les couleurs.
Metallisches Grau an den Wänden und an der Decke ist die neue, neutrale Farbe, die gut zu allen anderen passt.

07 A ceiling covered with wood tends to make a room look smaller, so it is best to paint the walls in white or pale colors.
Les plafonds revêtus de bois tendent à réduire visuellement la taille de la pièce. Privilégier alors les murs peints en couleurs claires.
Mit Holz verkleidete Decken reduzieren visuell die Größe des Raums.

Deshalb ist es empfehlenswert, die Wände weiß oder in hellen Farben zu streichen.

008 The alternation of pink and lilac walls establishes a bright, modern feel.
L'alternance de murs peints en rose et mauve crée une ambiance moderne et lumineuse.
Durch abwechselnd rosa und lila gestrichene Wände entsteht eine moderne und helle Wohnumgebung.

009 A rectangular room looks bigger if the narrow walls are painted with paler colors than the long ones.
Pour agrandir visuellement une pièce rectangulaire, peindre les murs plus étroits de couleurs plus claires, et choisir des tons plus sombres pour les autres.
Um einen rechteckigen Raum visuell größer wirken zu lassen, ist es ausreichend, die schmalen Wände in helleren Farben und die übrigen in dunkleren Tönen zu streichen.

010 Bathroom and kitchen tiles can be substituted by plastic paint, as this keeps out dampness and offers a wider range of colors.
Les carrelages de salles de bains et cuisines peuvent être remplacés par des peintures plastiques. Elles isolent de l'humidité et se déclinent dans un nuancier plus haut en couleurs.
Die Badezimmer- und Küchenkacheln können durch normale Plastikfarbe ersetzt werden, die die Feuchtigkeit fern hält und mehr Möglichkeiten für die farbliche Gestaltung bietet.

© Joan Roig

© Tres Tintas BCN

© Veruso

© Tapeten Agentur

© Extratapete

011 A wall-size photo or illustration printed on a sheet of paper does not take up any space and provides sufficient decoration for a small room.
Une photo ou une illustration imprimée sur papier mural occupe peu de place et décore à elle seule une petite pièce.
Ein Foto oder eine auf Papier gedruckte Zeichnung in der Größe einer Wand nimmt keinen Platz weg und reicht als Dekoration eines kleinen Zimmers aus.

012 A succession of strongly contrasting, uniformly colored motifs can highlight different settings in a small room.
Une série de motifs bien distincts, tout en restant dans les mêmes nuances de tons, façonne des univers différents dans un petit espace de vie.
Die Aufeinanderfolge unterschiedlicher Motive in den gleichen Farbtönen lässt verschiedene Umgebungen in einem kleinen Raum entstehen.

013 Op-Art graphics help to blur the outlines of walls and make spaces look bigger.
Les graphiques optiques aident à estomper les angles des murs et par la même à agrandir l'espace.
Optische Grafiken lassen die Begrenzung durch die Wände verschwinden und vergrößern deshalb visuell den Raum.

© Tres Tintas BCN

4 Brightly colored designs set against pale backgrounds are ideal for dark spaces.
Les motifs de couleurs vives sur fond clair sont parfaits dans les espaces sombres.
Motive in kräftigen Farben auf hellem Untergrund eignen sich ideal für dunkle Räume.

5 Textured white or silver wallpaper helps to reflect light.
Les papiers peints texturés blanc ou argent permettent de refléter la lumière.
Strukturtapeten in Weiß oder Silber reflektieren das Licht.

6 Walls look bigger if they are divided horizontally by two types of paper with different designs and contrasting colors.
Les murs paraissent plus grands s'ils sont divisés horizontalement par deux papiers peints aux motifs différents et aux teintes contrastées.
Die Wände wirken größer, wenn sie horizontal durch Tapeten mit verschiedenen Motiven und Kontrastfarben unterteilt werden.

7 Contrasting graphic motifs are ideal for vinyl wallpaper in kitchens.
Les motifs graphiques contrastés sont parfaits pour les papiers vinyles de la cuisine.
Kontrastierende grafische Motive eignen sich ideal für Vinyltapeten in Küchen.

018 In order to avoid visually overloading a room, it is advisable to put wallpaper on just one wall and paint the remainder in a complementary color.
Pour ne pas écraser la pièce, préférer l'application d'un papier peint sur un seul mur et peindre les autres dans une couleur complémentaire.
Damit der Raum nicht überladen wirkt, ist es besser, nur eine Wand zu tapezieren. Die anderen streicht man in einer Komplementärfarbe.

019 A single wall with stripes that continue on to the ceiling serves to make corridors or very narrow rooms appear longer. It is important for the adjoining walls to be white or painted in a complementary color.
Un seul mur habillé de rayures qui se prolongent sur le plafond permet d'agrandir les couloirs ou les pièces très étroites. Il est important que les murs contigus soient blancs ou dans une teinte complémentaire.
Wenn man eine Wand mit einer gestreiften Tapete tapeziert und die Streifen an der Decke fortsetzt, werden Flure und sehr schmale Räume optisch verlängert. Wichtig ist, dass die angrenzenden Wände weiß oder in einer Komplementärfarbe gestrichen werden.

020 The latest trend is to cover a low piece of furniture with the same paper as the wall.
Actuellement, la tendance préconise de revêtir un ou deux meubles du même papier que celui du mur.
Der neuste Trend ist es, ein niedriges Möbelstück mit der gleichen Tapete zu tapezieren, die an der Wand verwendet wurde.

© Rupert Steine

© Gogortza & Llorella

021   Smooth wooden covering is ideal for minimalist houses, regardless of the size of the rooms.
Indépendamment de la taille des pièces, les habillages de bois lisse sont idéaux dans les maisons minimalistes.
Verkleidungen mit glattem Holz eignen sich ideal für minimalistische Häuser, egal welche Größe die Räume haben.

022   Ash and birch are particularly suited to small spaces, on account of their distinctive luminosity.
Pour les espaces réduits, il est judicieux de choisir le bois de hêtre ou de bouleau, réputés pour leur luminosité.
In kleineren Räumen ist die Verwendung von Buchen- oder Birkenholz empfehlenswert, weil diese Holzsorten sehr hell wirken.

023   If wood is knotted, it is best to paint or cover it with an opaque varnish to give it a modern look.
Si le bois présente des noeuds, le peindre ou le teinter dans une nuanc opaque pour conférer à l'espace une touche contemporaine.
Wenn das Holz Astlöcher hat, sollte man es mit Anstrichfarbe oder eine deckenden Farbbeize streichen, damit es moderner wirkt.

024   Rooms look bigger and brighter with whitewashed wood on the walls and a bright yellow or orange ceiling.
Pour que les pièces gagnent en amplitude et luminosité, peindre le boi du mur en blanc et le plafond en orange ou jaune intense.

Räume wirken weiter und heller, wenn das Holz an den Wänden weiß gestrichen ist, und die Decke in Orange oder intensivem Gelb.

25 Wooden strips create a sense of depth when they are arranged horizontally.
Des liteaux de bois placés horizontalement accentuent l'impression de profondeur.
Wenn man Holzleisten horizontal anbringt, wirkt der Raum tiefer.

26 It is best not to alter the natural wood color of friezes. Varnishes only look modern in very spacious settings.
Pour les frises, garder de préférence la couleur naturelle du bois. Le côté moderne des vernis n'est valable que dans les très grands espaces.
An den Friesen sollte man das Holz in seiner Naturfarbe belassen; Lackierungen wirken nur in sehr weiten Räumen zeitgemäß.

27 Wooden ceilings offset the dark characteristic of brick walls.
Les plafonds en bois tranchent sur l'obscurité des murs de brique.
Holzdecken eignen sich gut, um dunkle Ziegelwände auszugleichen.

28 Boards assembled to look like mosaics or tiles elegantly break up the monotony of wood.
Les panneaux à l'instar de mosaïques ou de carrelages, brisent tout en élégance, la monotonie du bois.

Holzplatten, die wie Mosaiken oder Kacheln angeordnet sind, unterbrechen die Monotonie des Holzes auf elegante Art.

029 False wooden ceilings can provide storage space if they are fitted with a hidden sliding entrance.
Les faux plafonds en bois peuvent servir d'espace de rangement : prévoir à cet effet une ouverture coulissante masquée.
Eingezogene, falsche Decken aus Holz schaffen Stauraum, wenn man eine versteckte Schiebetür anbringt.

030 Long wooden strips used to cover walls and ceilings can be curved at the joints to create an effect of continuity.
Pour créer un effet de continuité, on peut incurver les listels de bois qui courent sur les murs et plafonds jusque dans les angles.
Wenn man lange Holzleisten, die als Verkleidung der Wände und Decken dienen, an den Fugen krümmt, wirkt der Raum durchgehend.

© Bisazza

© Bisazza

© Bisazza

031   The latest designs of tiles allow mosaics to be installed in a sitting room, as they resemble wallpaper.
Grâce aux nouveaux designs, les carrelages prennent des allures de papiers peints, créant des mosaïques modernes qui peuvent s'appliquer au salon.
Es gibt moderne Mosaikkacheln in neuen Ausführungen, die Tapeten ähneln und sich deshalb gut für Wohnzimmer eignen.

032   Vitreous mosaics bring luminosity to bathrooms on account of their iridescence and the variety of shades contained in a single color.
Les mosaïques de pâte de verre irisée illuminent les salles de bains grâce au brillant de leur matière et à la riche palette de leur camaïeu de teintes.
Mit verglasten, schillernden Mosaikkacheln, die es in vielen verschiedenen Farbtönen gibt, kann man helle, ansprechende Badezimmer gestalten.

033   The latest designs take advantage of gold and silver mosaics to trace narrow lines – either horizontal or vertical – at any height on the wall.
La dernière tendance est d'intégrer des mosaïques dorées ou argentées pour créer des plinthes étroites à n'importe quelle hauteur du mur, à l'horizontale ou verticale.
Der neuste Trend ist es, goldene und silberne Mosaiken für schmale Zierstreifen in jeglicher Höhe an der Wand zu verwenden, sowohl in waagerechter als auch in senkrechter Richtung.

034   Recently launched ceramic tiles designed to imitate bamboo give settings a natural look.

© Bisazza

Les nouveaux revêtements de céramique, imitant le bambou, créent des ambiances naturelles.
Die neuen Keramikverkleidungen, die Bambus imitieren, lassen die Wohnumgebung natürlich wirken.

5   An old kitchen can acquire a very contemporary look if areas with traditional tiles are combined with other sections painted in contrasting matt colors.
Les cuisines anciennes jouent la modernité en associant des panneaux de céramiques traditionnelles à d'autres carreaux aux tons contrastés et d'aspect mat.
Alte Küchen wirken sehr modern, wenn man die Bereiche mit traditionellen Küchenfliesen mit anderen Flächen kombiniert, die in matten Kontrastfarben gestrichen sind.

6   The combination of colors to create designs or checkerboard formations on walls has gone out of style, and also overloads a space visually.
L'association de couleurs, formant des motifs ou des damiers, n'est plus de mise pour les murs : cela crée un univers trop chargé.
Kombinationen an den Wänden in Farben, die Motive oder Schachbrettmuster bilden, sind nicht mehr modern und lassen den Raum visuell überladen wirken.

7   To make small bathrooms look bigger, they must be covered with large, pale-colored tiles with no borders.

Pour agrandir les petites salles de bains, préférer un habillage à base de grands carreaux clairs, sans frises.
Kleine Bäder wirken größer, wenn man sie mit großen Kacheln in hellen Tönen ohne Zierstreifen verkleidet.

038   A sense of spaciousness can be achieved by using uninterrupted expanses of color, so tiles with designs are to be avoided.
Optimiser également la sensation d'espace grâce à des carreaux unis, en évitant les céramiques à motifs.
Durch volle Farben gewinnt man Raum, deshalb sollte man Kacheln mit Motiven vermeiden.

039   To give a kitchen or bathroom a modern look, choose medium-size, square tiles in a single color.
Ajouter une touche contemporaine à la salle de bains ou à la cuisine en choisissant des carreaux ou des carrelages carrés, de taille moyenne et de couleur unie.
Um eine Küche oder ein Bad zeitgemäß zu gestalten, wählen Sie Kacheln oder Fliesen mittlerer Größe in vollen Farben.

040   Rooms look larger when the same tiles are used on the walls and the floor.
Pour agrandir l'espace, il suffit d'employer le même carrelage sur le sol et les murs.
Räume wirken optisch größer, wenn die Wände mit den gleichen Fliesen verkleidet sind wie der Boden.

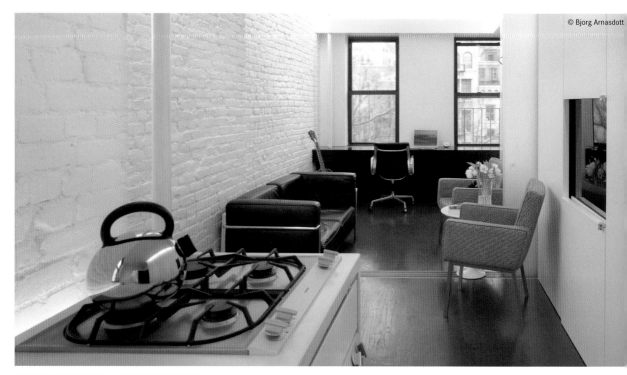

© Bjorg Arnasdott

© Andrea Martiradonna

041 A coat of white paint makes rooms with brick walls look spacious, counteracting the latter's tendency to have a darkening effect because their porous texture absorbs light.

Les murs de brique ont tendance à assombrir l'atmosphère car leur texture poreuse absorbe la lumière. Pour y pallier, les peindre en blanc et agrandir ainsi l'espace.

Ziegelwände lassen den Raum dunkler wirken, denn ihre poröse Textur absorbiert das Licht. Eine Schicht weiße Farbe lässt den Eindruck von Weite entstehen.

042 When brick ceilings or walls are adjacent to smooth surfaces, it is advisable to merge the two areas by using a range of pale colors.

Lorsque l'on conjugue plafonds ou murs de briques avec d'autres surfaces lisses, y associer, de préférence, une palette de couleurs claires.

Wenn Decken oder Wände aus Ziegelstein mit anderen glatten Flächen kombiniert werden, sollte man sich für helle Farbtöne entscheiden.

043 Vaulted brick ceilings require special upward lighting to make them less oppressive.

Les plafonds voûtés dans cette matière nécessitent un éclairage spéci orienté vers le haut pour diminuer la sensation d'oppression.

Für Decken mit Ziegelgewölben ist eine besondere Beleuchtung nach oben notwendig, damit sie nicht bedrückend wirken.

© Yael Pincus

4 White or ivory-colored organdy curtains lighten up rooms with brick walls.
Les rideaux d'organdi de couleur ivoire ou blanche allègent les pièces habillées de brique.
Gardinen aus naturweißem oder weißem Organdy lassen mit Ziegelstein verkleidete Räume freundlicher wirken.

5 Medium-size red bricks create the feeling of a loft-style environment.
Les briques de couleur rouge, de taille moyenne, créent une ambiance loft.
Durch rote Ziegel in mittleren Größen wirkt der Raum wie ein Loft.

6 Natural wooden furniture is the most appropriate complement for rooms dominated by brick.
Les meubles en bois naturel sont le meilleur allié des pièces habillées essentiellement de brique.
Möbel aus Naturholz lassen Räume mit Wänden aus Ziegelstein weniger düster wirken.

7 Brick should not be combined with rustic tiled floors.
Eviter de combiner la brique avec les sols en céramique rustique.
Man sollte Ziegel nicht mit rustikalen Bodenfliesen kombinieren.

8 Ceramic bricks are ideal for kitchens because they are extremely resistant to moisture.

De par leur résistance à l'humidité, les briques en céramique sont idéales pour la cuisine.
Keramikziegel eignen sich besonders gut für Küchen, weil sie feuchtigkeitsbeständig sind.

049 To create a contemporary look, make an arrangement of bricks in a range of metallic grays.
Pour créer une ambiance contemporaine, utiliser une composition de briques dans une palette de gris métallisés.
Um eine moderne Wohnumgebung zu schaffen, kann man Backsteine in metallischen Grautönen kombinieren.

050 Lighting must always be on the cold side, with small lamps that give an intense white light.
L'éclairage doit toujours tendre vers une ambiance froide, avec des petites lampes qui dégagent une lumière très blanche.
Die Beleuchtung sollte eher kalt sein; vorzugsweise sollte man Glühbirnen verwenden, die ein sehr weißes Licht ausstrahlen.

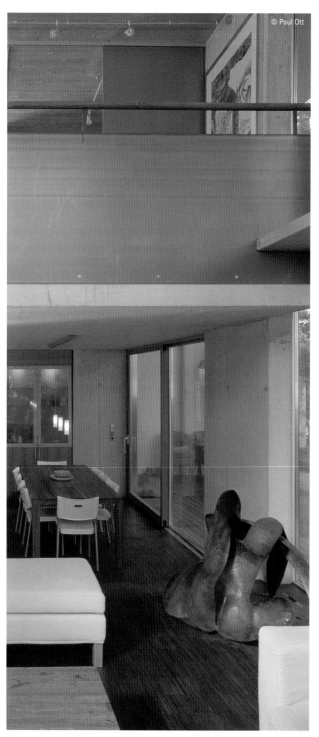

© Paul Ott

© Satoshi Okada Architect

© Pep Escoda

051 The inherent austerity of concrete is ideal for modern houses with an industrial look and very little furniture.
L'austérité caractéristique du béton en fait un matériau idéal pour les maisons modernes aux allures industrielles, dotées d'un mobilier restrein
Beton ist ein so schlichtes Material, dass es sich ausgezeichnet für moderne Häuser im industriellen Look mit wenig Möbeln eignet.

052 A room with ceilings and walls lined with uninterrupted concrete gains warmth when complemented by brightly colored natural fabrics.
Réchauffer l'ambiance des plafonds et murs en chapes de béton sans joints, à l'aide de tissus naturels de couleurs vives.
Räume mit einer Betonbeschichtung, ohne Fugen an den Decken und Wänden, wirken in Kombination mit natürlichen Textilien in kräftigen Farben wärmer.

053 Polished concrete looks good on both floors and walls. One surface ca be dyed to make the space seem bigger.
Le ciment ciré s'utilise aux étages comme sur les murs. Pour amplifier l'espace, il suffit de teindre certaines surfaces.
Zementglattstrich kann sowohl für den Boden als auch für die Wände verwendet werden. Um den Raum weiter wirken zu lassen, kann eine der Flächen getönt werden.

054 Rectangular recesses in exposed concrete walls can be used to hold shelves with brightly colored pottery vases of various shapes and sizes
Les alcôves rectangulaires, creusées dans les murs de béton brut,

peuvent servir d'étagères pour y poser des pots en céramique aux formes variées et de couleurs vives.
Rechteckige Öffnungen in unverputzten Betonwänden können als Regale für Keramikkrüge in verschiedenen Formen und kräftigen Farben verwendet werden.

55 Neo-baroque decorative details counteract the rigidity of exposed concrete.
Les détails de décoration néo-baroque tranchent sur la rigidité du béton.
Die neobarocken Dekorationselemente nehmen den unverputzten Betonflächen ihre Strenge.

56 Powdered plaster mixed with concrete produces a rustic texture and a color that not only looks modern but also adds luminosity.
La poudre de plâtre, mélangée au béton, produit une texture rustique et une couleur qui en plus d'une allure contemporaine, ajoute de la luminosité.
Wenn man Gipspulver mit Beton vermischt, erzielt man eine rustikale Textur und eine Farbe, die nicht nur zeitgemäß, sondern auch hell wirkt.

57 Another option is to apply a very watery layer of white paint on the concrete so that the latter's texture remains visible.
Penser à appliquer une touche de peinture blanche très aqueuse directement sur le béton pour que la texture reste apparente.
Eine andere Möglichkeit ist es, eine Schicht weiße, wasserlösliche Farbe direkt auf den Beton aufzutragen, so dass dessen Textur nicht verdeckt wird.

058 Polished concrete worktops give any bathroom or kitchen a minimalist touch.
Les plans de travail en béton ciré confèrent un aspect minimaliste à n'importe qu'elle cuisine ou salle de bains.
Arbeitsflächen aus poliertem Beton wirken in jedem Bad oder jeder Küche minimalistisch.

059 One of the latest design innovations consists of Litracon cement panels with incorporated optic fibers. The result is a thin but highly resistant wall covering studded with lights.
Les panneaux en ciment Litracon, à fibres optiques incorporées, sont une des dernières innovations. Le résultat est un mur avec des points lumineux, léger et très résistant à la fois.
Eine der letzten Innovationen sind Paneele aus transluzentem Beton Litracon, dem lichtleitende Glasfasern beigemischt sind. So entstehen lichtdurchlässige Wände, die sehr leicht wirken, aber gleichzeitig besonders widerstandsfähig sind.

060 In single-space homes shrouded in concrete, the kitchen area can stand out by covering it with matt steel.
Dans les maisons à ambiance unique revêtues de béton, délimiter l'espace de la cuisine en l'habillant d'acier patiné.
In Wohnumgebungen mit nur einem einzigen, mit Beton verkleideten Raum kann der Küchenbereich durch eine Stahlverkleidung mit matter Oberfläche abgegrenzt werden.

© Groep Delta Architectuur

© Eric Koyama

© Cathrine Tigh

061   All that is required to achieve a minimalist bathroom is a black slate surface and pale wooden covering.
Pour une salle de bain minimaliste, il suffit d'avoir un plan de travail en pierre d'ardoise noire et un habillage en bois clair.
Um ein Bad minimalistisch zu gestalten, genügen eine Ablage aus schwarzem Schiefer und eine Verkleidung aus hellem Holz.

062   White or beige marble with horizontal veins helps make a space look bigger.
Le marbre blanc ou beige doté de veines horizontales contribue à agrandir l'espace.
Weißer oder beiger Marmor mit horizontaler Maserung lässt den Raum größer wirken.

063   Large, polished granite panels create very luminous spaces. The latest trend is to combine them with straight-edged furniture.
Les grands panneaux de granit ciré créent des pièces très lumineuses. Les dernières tendances associent ces revêtements au mobilier de lignes droites.
Große Platten aus poliertem Granit machen die Räume sehr hell. Der neuste Trend ist diese Verkleidungen mit geradlinigen Möbeln zu kombinieren.

064   Pillars and small walls with openings can be covered with long but discreet stones with irregular surfaces.

© Trevor Main

Les colonnes et les petits murs dotés d'ouvertures peuvent être habillés de petites pierres longues, irrégulières sur la face frontale.
Säulen und kleine Wände mit Öffnungen können mit kleinen, länglichen Steinen mit unregelmäßiger Vorderfläche verkleidet werden.

065 Rustic-looking stone is the most appropriate covering for houses with exposed beams and mezzanines.
La pierre à l'état rustique est le revêtement idéal pour les maisons dotées de poutres et d'entresols métalliques apparents.
Rustikaler Naturstein ist die beste Verkleidung für Häuser mit sichtbaren Dachbalken und Zwischenetagen aus Metall.

066 When covering a wall with stone, it is best to stay within a single chromatic range.
Pour habiller un mur en pierre, préférer une même gamme chromatique.
Wenn man eine Wand mit Naturstein verkleidet, sollte man Steine in den gleichen Farbtönen wählen.

067 Settings covered with sheets of slate or marble take on a futuristic air with strong lighting hidden in the ceiling joints.
Pour que les espaces revêtus d'ardoise ou de marbre prennent des allures futuristes, y ajouter un éclairage puissant, dissimulé dans les joints du plafond.
Räume, die mit Schieferplatten oder Marmor verkleidet sind, wirken mit einer kräftigen Beleuchtung, welche die Deckenfugen verbirgt, futuristisch.

068 Any textured stone covering must be adjoined by a smooth surface.
Tout habillage en pierre texturée doit être adouci par un autre revêtement lisse.
Alle Flächen, die mit Steinen mit Textur verkleidet sind, sollten an glatte Flächen angrenzen.

069 Quartz finishings in strong colors like red, yellow or blue are very effective in bathrooms and kitchens.
Les finitions en quartz de couleurs intenses comme le rouge, jaune ou bleu, sont parfaites pour les salles de bains et cuisines.
Alle Flächen aus Quarz in intensiven Farben wie Rot, Gelb oder Blau eignen sich gut für Bäder und Küchen.

070 Natural-fiber fabrics help soften the coldness of stone.
Les tissus en fibre naturelle permettent d'adoucir la froideur de la pierre.
Textilien aus Naturfaser gleichen die Kälte des Steins aus.

© Volker Seding

© Volker Seding

071 Built-in kitchens can look bigger when covered with matt stainless steel which contrasts with the shiny finish of kitchen equipment.

Pour agrandir visuellement les cuisines américaines, choisir un habillage en acier inoxydable à l'aspect satiné, pour contraster avec le fini brillant de l'électroménager.

Um offene Küchen weiter wirken zu lassen, kann man sie mit mattem Edelstahl verkleiden, und mit glänzenden Haushaltsgeräten einen Kontrast schaffen.

072 A wall with glossy square stainless-steel panels creates interesting interplays of textures and is ideal for small settings with little furniture space.

Un mur de panneaux encadrés d'acier aux finitions cirées crée d'intéressants jeux de textures. Il est idéal pour des petits univers qui ne peuvent accueillir un grand nombre de meubles.

Eine Wand mit quadratischen, polierten Stahlplatten lässt interessante Spiele mit der Textur entstehen. Ideal für kleine Räume, in die nur wenig Möbel passen.

073 Iron adds an industrial touch that combines very well with exposed concrete and brick.

Le fer donne un look industriel qui se marie à merveille avec le béton apparent et la brique.

Eisen lässt den Raum industriell wirken und passt gut zu unverputztem Beton und Ziegelstein.

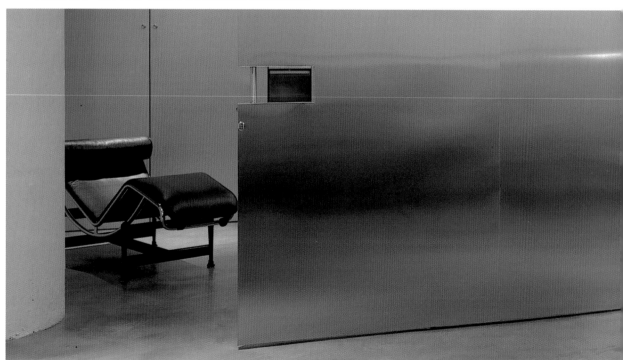

074 Copper sheets create a warm atmosphere. They are perfect for a wall in a bedroom or sitting room.
Les plaques de cuivre créent une atmosphère chaleureuse. Elles sont parfaites pour le mur d'une chambre à coucher ou du salon.
Kupferblech macht den Raum warm und freundlich. Ideal für Schlafzimmer- und Wohnzimmerwände.

075 A sheet of galvanized steel on a ceiling can be curved to be extended as a wall.
La plaque d'acier qui habille le plafond peut être incurvée pour se prolonger ensuite, à l'instar d'un mur.
Ein Blechstreifen aus verzinktem Stahl an der Decke kann gekrümmt und an der Wand weitergeführt werden.

076 Fluorescent lighting provides stimulating settings in spaces covered in metal.
Les espaces habillés de métal irradient une lumière fluorescente qui crée des ambiances spéciales.
Leuchtstoffröhren lassen mit Metall verkleidete Räume sehr ansprechend wirken.

077 Zinc is particularly appropriate for covering construction elements like beams.
Le zinc est idéal pour habiller les détails de construction comme les poutres.
Zink eignet sich zur Verkleidung von Konstruktionselementen wie Balken.

078 A less radical option is to mark out small spaces on a wall and floor with adhesive paper that imitates aluminum.
Une autre possibilité, moins radicale, est de délimiter des petits espaces dans le mur et le sol à l'aide de papiers adhésifs qui imitent l'aluminium.
Eine weniger radikale Möglichkeit ist kleinere Bereiche der Wand und des Bodens mit Klebefolie zu begrenzen, die Aluminium imitiert.

079 Retro-style furniture in white or red provides an ideal contrast to metallic settings.
Les meubles de style rétro, blancs ou rouges, affichent un contraste idéal dans les ambiances métallisées.
Weiße und rote Möbel im Retrostil bilden einen idealen Kontrast in Wohnumgebungen mit viel Metall.

080 If a house has a central partition that distributes the various spaces, this divider can be covered in dark metal while the adjacent rooms can be painted pure white.
Si la maison dispose d'une cloison centrale qui distribue les espaces, privilégier un revêtement en métal foncé et peindre le reste des pièces en blanc pur.
Wenn es in der Wohnung eine zentrale Trennwand gibt, welche die Räume unterteilt, kann man diese mit dunklem Metall verkleiden und die übrigen Räume in reinem Weiß streichen.

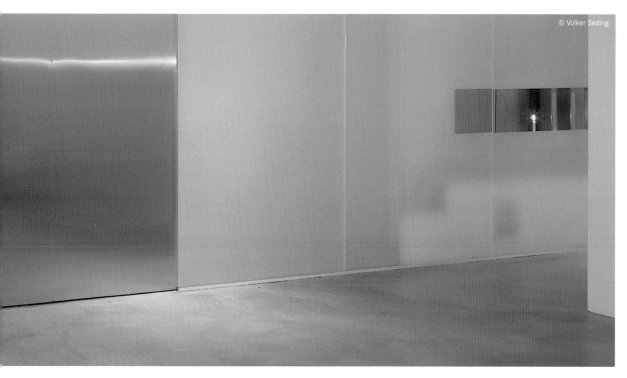

© Volker Seding

© Jordi Miralles

© Jaime Navarro

081 If the ceiling in a narrow corridor is replaced by double glazing, sunshine can filter into all the rooms of a house.
En remplaçant le plafond d'un couloir étroit par une double plaque de verre, la lumière naturelle s'irradie dans toutes les pièces de la maison.
Wenn man die Decke von engen Fluren durch eine doppelte Glasscheib ersetzt, scheint das Tageslicht in alle Räume des Hauses durch.

082 Glass bricks allow light to pass into even the darkest of rooms.
Les pavés de verre permettent de filtrer la lumière vers les pièces plus sombres.
Glasziegel lassen das Licht in die dunkelsten Räume durch.

083 Windows with thermal insulation make it possible to insert openings stretching along an entire wall and thus merge an indoor setting with the exterior.
Les vitres à isolation thermique permettent des ouvertures de la taille du mur entier, intégrant ainsi l'univers intérieur avec l'extérieur.
Die Verwendung von Isolierglas ermöglicht Fenster, die eine ganze Wan einnehmen und so innen und außen miteinander verbinden.

084 A rectangular opening above a washbasin allows light to penetrate inside from overhead, creating a very attractive effect.
Un puits de lumière rectangulaire au dessus d'une vasque crée une lumière zénithale irradiant une atmosphère des plus agréables.
Ein rechteckiges Fenster über dem Waschbecken lässt das Licht von oben einfallen, wodurch eine einladende Atmosphäre entsteht.

© Gogortza & Llorella

© Hisao Suzuki

85 A series of bottom-hung windows is perfect for making a space with an attic ceiling appear bigger.
Les espaces aux plafonds mansardés gagnent de l'ampleur grâce à une série de fenêtres oscillo-battantes.
Um Dachzimmer mit schrägen Decken weiter wirken zu lassen, eignen sich Sequenzen aus Kippfenstern sehr gut.

86 Colored glass mosaics can be used to reproduce a Pop-Art style illustration spread across an entire wall.
Les mosaïques de verre permettent de reproduire des illustrations Pop Art pour en habiller le mur.
Mit Mosaiken aus buntem Kristall kann man ein Pop-Art-Bild auf einer ganzen Wand nachbilden.

87 A setting can be transformed through the addition of a glass enclosure for a balcony or back yard.
Une verrière installée sur un balcon ou un patio crée un nouvel univers.
Durch Glasverkleidungen an Balkonen oder Innenhöfen entstehen neue Räume.

88 Glass treated with acid is ideal for closing off bathrooms integrated into another room, as it allows light to enter while still guaranteeing privacy.
Le verre gravé est une solution idéale pour clore les salles de bains intégrées à la chambre : il filtre la lumière tout en préservant l'intimité.

Geätztes Glas eignet sich ausgezeichnet, um Bäder zu schließen, die in einen Raum integriert sind. Dieses Glas lässt das Licht durch, verhindert aber Durchblicke.

089 Curved tempered glass makes it possible to install small domes and create internal patios.
Le verre trempé arrondi permet d'installer des petites coupoles pour créer des patios intérieurs.
Gekrümmtes, gehärtetes Glas eignet sich für kleine Kuppeln über Innenhöfen.

090 Laminated glass floors are an option for mezzanines as they prevent a space from being visually obstructed.
Les sols en verre laminé s'installent dans les mezzanines car ils évitent une obstruction visuelle de l'espace.
Böden aus gewalztem Glas sind aufgrund ihrer Transparenz eine gute Lösung für Zwischengeschosse, weil sie die Räume visuell nicht begrenzen.

Floors
Sols
Bodenbeläge

Floors in the same material and color as the walls and ceilings help to make a space look bigger. When different materials and colors are combined, however, they produce visual effects that redefine settings beyond their architectural configuration. From the elegant coolness of stone to the warmth of carpets with natural fibers, flooring turns a room into a small microcosm governed by its own rules.

Employer les mêmes matériaux et couleurs au sol, sur les murs et plafonds permet d'agrandir l'espace. Cependant, la combinaison de différents tons et matières provoque des effets visuels qui redéfinissent les univers au-delà de leur architecture. De la froideur élégante de la pierre à la chaleur des fibres naturelles des tapis, les sols transforment chaque pièce en un mini univers qui obéit à ses propres règles.

Böden aus dem gleichen Material und in der gleichen Farbe wie die Wände und Decken vergrößern den Raum visuell. Wenn man jedoch Farbtöne und Materialien an den Wänden und der Decke kombiniert, entstehen optische Effekte, welche die Wohnumgebung noch über die architektonischen Elemente hinausgehend neu definieren. Die verschiedenen Typen von Verkleidungen, wie zum Beispiel der elegante und kalte Stein und die warmen Naturfasern von Teppichen, verwandeln jeden Raum in ein kleines Universum, in dem eigene Regeln gelten.

© Nuria Fuentes

© Guy Wenborne

© Gogortza & Llorella

091 Carpets in natural colors enlarge a space visually. If they are covered with small rugs in contrasting colors, they establish different settings.
Les moquettes de couleur écrue agrandissent l'espace. Créer différentes ambiances en y ajoutant des petits tapis aux couleurs contrastées.
Teppichböden in Naturtönen lassen den Raum weiter wirken. Wenn ma auf diese Teppichböden kleine Teppiche in Kontrastfarben legt, entstehen verschiedene Bereiche.

092 Prints with large geometric motifs are suitable for small spaces.
Les petits espaces seront mieux mis en valeur par des imprimés aux grands motifs géométriques.
Drucke mit großen geometrischen Motiven eignen sich für kleinere Räume.

093 Carpets with horizontal stripes help make narrow passageways look wider.
Les tapis aux rayures horizontales élargissent les couloirs étroits.
Teppiche mit horizontalen Streifen lassen enge Flure weiter wirken.

094 Furrowed mats woven with natural fibers like jute and sisal combine very well with floors made of wood, concrete or brick.
Les fibres naturelles de texture cannelée, comme le jute ou le sisal, se marient à merveille avec un carrelage de bois, béton ou brique.
Gerillte Naturfasern wie Jute und Sisal passen gut zu Böden aus Holz, Beton und Backstein.

© Ángel Baltanás

5 Small round rugs in unbroken colors can easily be adapted to small spaces.
Les petits espaces apprivoisent facilement les petits tapis ronds de couleurs denses.
Kleine runde Teppiche in vollen Farben eignen sich ausgezeichnet für kleinere Räume.

6 Dark tiled floors should always be matched with woolen rugs in a natural color or a very pale beige.
Les dallages de céramique foncée s'accommodent parfaitement de tapis de laine écrue ou beige très clair.
Für dunkle Keramikböden eignen sich nur Wollteppiche in Naturweiß oder sehr hellem Beige.

7 Sitting rooms with predominantly black and brown furnishings can be enlivened by mauve or pink rugs.
Les salons, dont le mobilier affiche des tons dominants de marron et noir, s'illuminent au contact de la couleur mauve ou rose.
Wohnzimmer, in denen die Farben Braun und Schwarz bei den Möbeln vorherrschen, bekommen durch blasslila oder rosa Teppiche mehr Licht.

8 The so-called cow's horns (or black-and-white zebra's horns) are an elegant option for small sitting rooms.
Dans les petits salons, les cuirs de vache ou de zèbre, noirs et blancs, sont autant de touches élégantes.
Die so genannten Kuh- oder Zebrafelle in Schwarzweiß sind eine elegante Lösung für kleine Wohnzimmer.

099 Large, ethnic-style carpets with elaborate designs overpower a small space, so they should be avoided.
Eviter les grands tapis de style ethnique ou aux graphiques complexes, car ils sont trop chargés.
Große Teppiche im Ethnostil oder mit komplizierten Grafiken lassen eine Wohnumgebung schnell überladen wirken, deshalb sollte man sie lieber vermeiden.

100 Round carpets with concentric circles are ideal for marking the boundaries of a sitting room in a home confined to a single space.
Les tapis ronds dotés de cercles concentriques délimitent à merveille le salon dans une maison à espace unique.
Runde Teppiche mit konzentrischen Kreisen eignen sich gut, um ein Wohnzimmer in einer Wohnung mit nur einem Raum abzugrenzen.

© Eric Koyama

© Satoshi Okada Architects

101 Parquet is the most practical technique for installing a wooden floor th
requires no construction work.
Le parquet flottant est très pratique pour installer un plancher sans tr
de travaux.
Fertigparkett ist eine praktische Lösung, wenn man einen Holzboden
ohne aufwendige Bauarbeiten verlegen will.

102 Pale woods like maple and ash make rooms look bigger.
Les bois clairs, tel l'érable ou le hêtre, agrandissent les pièces.
Helles Holz wie Ahorn oder Buche lässt die Räume größer wirken.

103 Rather than using dark woods such as oak and walnut, it is preferable
stain parquet black and contrast it with walls in an ivory, anthracite-gr
or beige color.
Au lieu d'utiliser des bois sombres comme le chêne ou le noyer, teindr
de préférence le parquet dans un noir uni et le contraster par des mur
ivoire, gris anthracite ou beige.
Vor der Benutzung von dunklen Hölzern wie Eiche oder Nussbaum ist
besser, das Parkett ganz schwarz zu färben und die Wände naturweiß,
anthrazit oder beige zu streichen.

104 Flooring is available with pieces which, for the sake of greater
convenience, fit together like a jigsaw (the click system), thus avoiding
the need for glue.

© Ake Eson Lindman

Pour une pose plus facile, certains parquets sont constitués de morceaux qui s'assemblent comme les pièces d'un puzzle (système clic), sans avoir besoin d'être collés.
Noch einfacher zu verlegen ist das so genannte Klickparkett, bei dem die einzelnen Teile wie ein Puzzle ohne Verleimen miteinander verbunden werden.

A modern classic for small rooms is the combination of wooden floors and alternating scarlet and white walls.
Dans les petits espaces, la pose de parquets associés à des murs alternant le rouge et le blanc, est une méthode classique et moderne.
Ein moderner Klassiker für kleine Räume sind Holzböden, die abwechselnd mit scharlachroten und weißen Wänden kombiniert werden.

Straight lines give floors a stylish flourish. Mosaics with geometrical motifs are not recommended in small rooms.
Les lignes droites permettent de styliser le sol. Dans des petites pièces, éviter d'habiller les murs de mosaïques pour créer des motifs géométriques.
Gerade Linien machen den Boden sehr stilvoll. Es ist nicht empfehlenswert, in kleinen Räumen Mosaike zu verwenden, um geometrische Motive zu schaffen.

The use of whole wooden planks makes floors look bigger.

Le bois artisanal en listels continus agrandit visuellement les sols.
Bauholz in Leisten als Bodenbelag vergrößert den Raum visuell.

108 Wood in strong reddish colors has come back into fashion. This makes for original flooring, but it should be offset by very pale furniture.
Le bois aux tonalités de rouge intense est de nouveau de mise. Ce revêtement original doit être, toutefois, contrebalancé par des meubles aux tons clairs.
Holz in rötlichen Tönen liegt wieder im Trend. Bei diesem originellen Bodenbelag sollte man jedoch zum Ausgleich Möbel in sehr hellen Tönen wählen.

109 The synthetic insulation processes now applied to wood make it possible to put a wooden floor in a bathroom, similar to Nordic saunas.
Les processus d'isolement synthétique du bois permettent d'oser la pose d'un parquet dans la salle d'eau, à l'image des saunas nordiques.
Aufgrund der synthetischen Isolierung von Holz ist es möglich, im Bad einen Holzfußboden im Stile nordischer Saunen zu montieren.

110 Cork is a very warm and inviting natural material that can be used on both floors and walls, either untreated or varnished.
Le liège est une matière neutre très accueillante et chaude, qui, vernie ou à l'état brut, habille à merveille murs et sols.
Kork ist ein natürliches Material, das sehr warm und angenehm ist, sowohl lackiert als auch unbehandelt, und man kann es für Böden und für Wände verwenden.

© Shania Shegedyn

49

© Bisaz

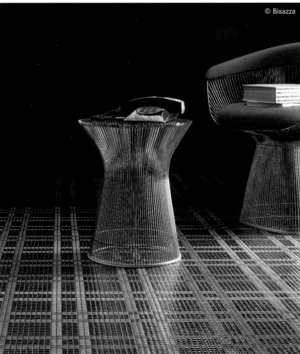

© Bisazza

111   Small houses with integrated settings can be made to look bigger wit
the placement of a single continuous ceramic flooring (with no joints)
Pour agrandir visuellement les petites maisons à espace unique, utilis
un seul carrelage en céramique continu et sans joints.
Kleine Häuser mit nur einem einzigen Raum wirken größer, wenn man
einen einzigen durchgehenden Bodenbelag aus Keramik wählt (ohne
Fugen).

112   Floors with a black-and-white checkerboard pattern can elegantly def
both bathrooms and kitchens.
Les sols en damier blanc et noir confèrent élégance aux cuisines et
salles de bain.
Böden mit schwarzweißem Schachbrettmuster definieren auf elegant
Weise Bäder und Küchen.

113   Large, polished square tiles are ideal for small sitting rooms as they
increase the sense of spaciousness.
Dans les petits salons, les larges carreaux, carrés et vitrifiés sont idé
pour agrandir l'espace.
Große, quadratische, glänzende Fliesen eignen sich ausgezeichnet für
kleine Wohnzimmer, die sie optisch vergrößern.

114   A corridor is transformed into a minimalist walkway if it is
complemented by a strip of gray or black tiles combined with LED
spotlights.
Pour transformer le couloir en une passerelle minimaliste, appliquer

© Bisazza

© Pep Escoda

une rangée de carreaux noirs ou gris associés à des spots LED.

Der Flur wird zu einem minimalistischen Laufsteg, wenn eine Reihe schwarzer oder grauer Fliesen mit LED-Strahlern kombiniert werden.

The latest trend is for clean-cut settings with strong contrasts, such as floors and walls covered with titanium-anthracite tiles offset by white furniture.

Les dernières tendances en vogue, prônent les ambiances épurées et contrastées, qui déclinent des sols et murs revêtus de carreaux de céramique de couleur titane anthracite, associés à des meubles blancs.

Der neuste Trend geht in Richtung reine und kontrastierte Wohnumgebungen, wie sie durch Böden und Wände entstehen, die mit titanfarbenen, anthrazitgrauen Fliesen verkleidet sind, in Kombination mit weißen Möbeln.

A modern home has no use for baseboards, as they are out of date and reduce wall space.

Dans une maison contemporaine, bannir les plinthes qui ne correspondent plus au goût du jour et rapetissent les murs.

In einem modernen Haus gibt es keine Sockel. Sie sind nicht mehr zeitgemäß und lassen die Wände kleiner wirken.

Traditional decorative edgings with plant motifs can be replaced by more modern variants with inscriptions in the style of conceptual art.

Les frises traditionnelles aux motifs végétaux peuvent être remplacées par d'autres plus modernes, avec un graphisme design.

Traditionelle dekorative Zierleisten mit Pflanzenmotiven werden durch modernere ersetzt, die Muster im Stil der Konzeptkunst aufweisen.

118 Mosaics in strong, bright colors like orange and yellow add luminosity and a cutting-edge feel to narrow, rectangular kitchens.

Les mosaïques aux couleurs fortes et vives, tels l'orange ou le jaune, apportent luminosité et une touche avant-gardiste aux cuisines étroites de forme rectangulaire.

Mosaiken in starken, lebendigen Farben wie Orange und Gelb lassen enge, rechteckige Küchen moderner und heller wirken.

119 Tiles imitating wood can bestow the latter's warmth in damp areas like the bathroom and kitchen.

Les carreaux de céramique, imitation bois, recréent la chaleur de cette matière dans des zones humides comme les salles d'eau et la cuisine.

Kacheln, die Holz imitieren, machen es möglich, dieses warme Material in feuchte Bereiche wie das Bad und die Küche einzubringen.

120 An original option for a child's bedroom is the application of tiles with invisible joints, in strips at least 3 ft wide in complementary colors.

Ajouter une touche d'originalité aux chambres d'enfants est facile : appliquer des carreaux sans joints, en frise d'au moins un mètre de large, dotée de couleurs complémentaires.

Eine originelle Lösung für das Kinderzimmer sind mindestens einen Meter lange Fliesen mit unsichtbaren Fugen in Komplementärfarben.

© Nelson Ko

© Nelson Ko

© Matteo Piazza

© Matteo Piazza

© Trevor Main

© Joan Mundó

© Luuk Kram

© Satoshi Okada Architects

121 Marble provides exceptional luminosity. For its majesticness to take
effect in small homes, it should be the sole covering in all the rooms.
Le marbre apporte une luminosité exceptionnelle. Il revêt des allures
majestueuses dans les petites pièces, à condition d'en être le matéria
unique.
Marmor ist ein besonders helles Material. Damit es in kleinen Häuser
wirklich seine Pracht entfalten kann, sollte es die einzige Verkleidung
allen Räumen sein.

122 A floor with black slate tiles sets the tone for an entire room, so it
should be complemented by white walls and furnishings in both color
Associer des dalles de pierre noire au sol à des murs blancs et un
mobilier dans les deux couleurs, donne du caractère à toute une pièc
Fußbodenplatten aus schwarzem Schiefer bestimmen den Charakter
des gesamten Raumes, deshalb sollten die Wände weiß sein und die
Möbel beide Farben haben.

123 A bathroom with natural-stone mosaics stretching to the shower
achieves unity and a sense of spaciousness. In such cases, the partiti
must be made of transparent glass.
Unifier les surfaces et les agrandir peut se faire en habillant la baigno
et la douche d'une mosaïque de pierres naturelles. Dans ce cas,
privilégier un pare-douche en verre transparent.
Bäder mit Mosaiken aus Naturstein, die bis zur Dusche reichen, wirke
sehr einheitlich und geräumig. Die Glastür der Dusche sollte in diesem
Fall transparent sein.

© Trevor Main

4 Heavily veined stone is appropriate for large spaces, but small homes are more suited to tiles in unbroken colors.
La pierre veinée est préconisée pour les grands espaces. Par contre, dans les petites pièces, préférer des carreaux lisses.
Steine mit starker Marmorierung eignen sich gut als Verkleidung großer Flächen. In kleinen Häusern ist es besser, glatte Platten zu verwenden.

5 A polished stone floor helps to make rooms with brick walls seem bigger.
La pierre cirée permet d'agrandir les pièces dotées de murs de brique.
Polierter Stein vergrößert Räume mit Ziegelwänden visuell.

6 Fifties-style furniture in white and natural wood is the best complement for granite floors.
Les meubles dans le style des années cinquante, associant le blanc et le bois naturel, sont le meilleur allié des espaces au sol de granit.
Weiße Möbel aus Naturholz im Stil der Fünfzigerjahre passen ausgezeichnet zu Granitfußböden.

7 Tables made of gray stone and glass blend into stoneware floors, and the resulting textural uniformity gives the impression of greater spaciousness.
Les tables associant la pierre grise et le verre permettent d'intégrer les sols de grès, l'uniformité de la texture accentuant la sensation d'espace.
Tische aus grauem Stein und Glas scheinen sich in Böden aus Steingut zu integrieren. Durch diese einheitliche Textur entsteht der Eindruck von mehr Weite.

128 A wide diagonal strip of white marble makes a room seem longer when it is set in a beige marble floor.
Une large bande de marbre blanc, posée en diagonale sur un sol de marbre beige, agrandit l'espace.
Eine breite diagonale Linie aus weißem Marmor auf dem Boden aus beigem Marmor verlängert die Räume.

129 It is advisable for staircases to be covered with the same stone as the floor, in order to avoid visually dividing the setting.
Pour éviter de casser l'ambiance générale, préférer le même revêtement en pierre pour les escaliers et le sol.
Man sollte die Treppen mit dem gleichen Material verkleiden wie den Fußboden, damit sie den Raum nicht visuell unterbrechen.

130 If the top of the washbasin unit is made of polished stone, a large mirror of the same size can double the apparent dimensions of a bathroom.
Un grand miroir de la taille du plan de toilette décuple l'espace de la salle de bains, si elle est en pierre cirée.
Ein großer Spiegel in der Größe der Ablage aus poliertem Stein kann die Größe des Raums des Bades zu verdoppeln.

© Trevor Main

© Guy Wenborne

© Leven Betts Studio

© Luuk Krame

© Guy Wenborne

131 Polished concrete floors make spaces look bigger on account of their sheen and the lack of joints.

Grâce à son éclat et à l'absence de joints, le ciment lisse posé sur les sols agrandit l'espace.

Mit ihrem Glanz und aufgrund der fehlenden Fugen vergrößern Böden aus Zementglattstrich den Raum visuell.

132 A concrete floor can be stained in different colors to mark off the various areas in a loft-style apartment.

Pour différencier les pièces d'un appartement style loft, teindre le ciment dans différentes teintes.

Um die verschiedenen Wohnbereiche im Stil einer Fabriketage zu unterscheiden, können verschiedene Farbtöne für den Zementboden gewählt werden.

133 Concrete with a matt finish comes to life with the addition of long-pile rugs in a contrasting color.

Le ciment d'aspect mat revit s'il est associé à des tapis aux couleurs contrastées et à poils longs.

Zement mit einer matten Oberfläche wirkt lebendiger mit langhaarigen Teppichen in Kontrastfarben.

134 One modern approach to a bathroom consists of covering it completely with strongly colored concrete and then adding a washbasin unit with a black wooden top.

© Guy Wenborne

Une autre façon de donner une touche contemporaine à la salle de bains est de l'habiller entièrement en ciment de couleur forte et de poser un plan de toilette en bois noir.
Eine zeitgemäße Option für das Bad ist es, dieses vollständig mit Zement in einer intensiven Farbe zu verkleiden und eine schwarze Ablage zu konstruieren.

5 Strips of concrete create a state-of-the-art look, when applied to floors, walls or ceilings.
Les listels de béton, appliqués à la fois sur le sol, les murs et le plafond, créent un univers avant-gardiste.
Betonlatten an den Wänden und Decken schaffen eine avantgardistische Wohnumgebung.

6 Rooms lined with exposed concrete need a significant supply of sunlight for much of the day.
Les pièces habillées de béton brut nécessitent un grand apport de lumière naturelle pendant la plus grande partie de la journée.
Räume, die mit unverputztem Beton verkleidet sind, sollten den größten Teil des Tages viel Licht von draußen erhalten.

7 The ideal lighting for this type of floor is a designer version of white fluorescent tubes.
l'éclairage idéal pour ce genre de revêtement est une version design de néons blancs.

Die beste Beleuchtung für diese Art von Verkleidungen sind interessant gestaltete, weiße Leuchtstofflampen.

138 Exposed concrete floors look more expansive in settings with contrasting white walls or steel panels.
Les sols de béton brut paraissent plus grands dans les espaces de vie habillés de panneaux d'acier ou en contraste avec des murs blancs.
Böden aus unverputztem Beton lassen Räume mit Stahlplatten an den Wänden oder weißen Wänden größer wirken.

139 Polished concrete floors and exposed iron beams are the perfect mix for giving a house an industrial feel.
Pour donner un air industriel à la maison, l'idéal est de combiner les sols de ciment lisse et de béton avec des poutres apparentes en fer.
Um einer Wohnung einen industriellen Touch zu geben, kann man Böden mit Zementglattstrich mit sichtbaren Eisenträgern kombinieren.

140 The use of ash wood in a ceiling makes rooms with a concrete floor seem more spacious.
Un habillage en bois de hêtre au plafond agrandit les pièces avec sol en ciment.
Buchenholz an der Decke lässt Räume mit Zementboden weiter wirken.

© Guy Wenborne

141 Vinyl flooring with vibrant colors and shiny surfaces are coming back into fashion.

Les revêtements de sol en vinyle, aux couleurs gaies et surfaces brillantes, ont le vent en poupe.

Vinylböden in kräftigen Farben und mit glänzenden Oberflächen sind wieder modern.

142 PVC floors printed with large-scale designs are ideal for widening the appearance of spaces such as corridors.

Les revêtements en PVC imprimés de grands motifs sont parfaits pour agrandir les espaces comme les couloirs.

Verkleidungen aus bedrucktem PVC mit großformatigen Mustern eigne sich hervorragend, um Flure weiter wirken zu lassen.

143 Resin finishes offer an alternative to polished concrete. They are easier to apply and come in brighter colors.

Les finitions en résine offrent une alternative au ciment poli. Elles sont plus faciles à installer et se déclinent dans une gamme de couleurs plu vives.

Verkleidungen aus Kunstharz stellen eine Alternative zum Zementglattstrich dar. Sie sind einfach anzubringen und haben lebendigere Farben.

144 A red floor gives a room a retro feel when combined with plastic furniture.

© Angelo Kaunat

Le sol de couleur rouge affiche un petit air rétro en association avec les meubles de plastique.
Rote Böden verleihen dem Raum einen gewissen Retrotouch, wenn sie mit Kunststoffmöbeln kombiniert werden.

145 A modern look can be created simply through the contrast between a wall painted turquoise and a pale brown PVC floor.
Le contraste entre un mur peint en turquoise et un sol revêtu de PVC marron clair imprime à l'ambiance un air de modernité.
Um moderne Wohnumgebungen zu schaffen, kann man eine Wand türkis streichen und einen Bodenbelag aus hellbraunem PVC wählen.

146 A child's room can be enlivened by strips of PVC in various colors.
Des frises en PVC de différentes couleurs donnent un air de fraîcheur aux chambres d'enfants.
Kinderzimmer wirken sehr frisch, wenn man sie mit PVC-Streifen in verschiedenen Farben dekoriert.

147 Resin sheets that imitate parquet are excellent for a kitchen floor because they are very easy to clean.
Les lattes de résine qui imitent le parquet conviennent à merveille aux sols de la cuisine pour leur facilité d'entretien.
Laminatfußböden aus Kunstharz, die Parkett imitieren, eignen sich sehr gut für Küchenböden, weil sie einfach zu reinigen sind.

148 Vinyl silhouettes give rise to original decorative schemes when they are applied to tiled floors.
Les images en vinyle découpées et appliquées sur les sols de céramique sont autant d'idées de décoration originales.
Wenn man Figuren aus Vinyl auf Keramikböden anbringt, entstehen interessante Effekte.

149 Vinyl laminates with graphic motifs can be extended from the floor to go up one of the walls in a kitchen where shelves have replaced closets.
Les laminés en vinyle dotés de motifs graphiques posés au sol peuvent se prolonger sur un des murs de la cuisine où les étagères se substituent aux placards.
Vinylplatten mit grafischen Motiven auf dem Boden können an einer der Küchenwände hochsteigen, an der die Schränke durch Regale ersetzt wurden.

150 These flooring elements can be cut to size in order to take the place of a rug.
Il est possible de découper ces revêtements à la taille d'un tapis.
Diese Verkleidungen können auf die Größe eines Teppichs zurechtgeschnitten werden.

Dividing and unifying elements
Éléments de partition et de décloisonnement
Trennende und vereinende Elemente

The layout of a home is crucial when it comes to winning back space. When the latter is at a premium, it is vital to take advantage of every nook and cranny by eliminating all unnecessary superfluity and assigning multiple functions to single elements. In the difficult balance between separating and joining, every structural component in a home can be exploited to the full; this results in solutions that are as creative as they are functional.

La distribution des pièces est essentielle pour gagner de l'espace. Lorsque chaque mètre carré compte, il faut tirer parti du moindre recoin de la maison, éliminer tout ce qui est superflu et attribuer des fonctions multiples à un seul élément. Dans cet équilibre fragile entre décloisonnement et cloisonnement, il faut optimiser chaque composante structurelle de la maison, grâce à des solutions aussi créatives que fonctionnelles.

Die Aufteilung der Räume spielt eine Schlüsselrolle, wenn man Platz gewinnen will. Wenn der Raum nicht besonders groß ist, muss man jeden Winkel einer Wohnung nutzen, alles eliminieren, was überflüssig ist und einem einzigen Element mehrere Funktionen zuordnen. Bei der Planung steht man vor der schwierigen Aufgabe, ein Gleichgewicht zwischen dem Trennen und dem Vereinen der einzelnen strukturellen Komponenten zu finden. Durch diese Herausforderung entstehen auch viele kreative und funktionelle Lösungen.

© Paul Ott

© Joan Roig

© Paskin Kyriakides Sands Architects

151 Windows with sliding panes are the best solution in terms of saving space. Other options include pivoting and folding panes, as well as sash windows in kitchens and bathrooms.

Les fenêtres aux vitres coulissantes occupent moins d'espace que d'autres. Pour les cuisines et salles de bains, les fenêtres à guillotines, les fenêtres pivotantes et repliables sont autant d'alternatives judicieuses.

Schiebefenster sparen viel Platz. Eine Alternative zu diesem System sin Vertikalschiebefenster für Küchen und Bäder, Schwingfenster und Klappfenster.

152 Window frames are not only less obtrusive when made of aluminum bu also allow more light to enter into the home.

Les profils d'aluminium allègent les cadres des fenêtres et permettent une arrivée de lumière plus importante.

Mit Aluminiumprofilen wirken die Fensterrahmen leichter und es fällt viel Tageslicht in den Raum.

153 Long, bottom-hung windows are ideally suited to sloping roofs.

Les fenêtres agrandies par une ouverture oscillo-battante sont idéales dans le cas de plafonds inclinés.

Längliche Drehkippfenster eignen sich ausgezeichnet für schräge Decken.

154 Wood trim requires windows with the same finish because any combination with another material would be overpowering.

© Shania Shegedyn

© Joan Mundó

Les habillages de bois requièrent des fenêtres du même fini. Les mélanger avec d'autres matériaux alourdit l'espace.
Bei Räumen mit Holzverkleidungen sollten auch die Fenster Holzrahmen haben. Wenn man andere Materialien benutzt, wirkt die Wohnung überladen.

155 Interior windows help to integrate different spaces and therefore make them seem bigger.
Les ouvertures sous forme de fenêtres intérieures permettent d'intégrer les espaces et se faisant de les agrandir.
Innere Fenster verbinden verschiedene Wohnbereiche und lassen sie deshalb größer wirken.

156 Glass or wood enclosures in back yards or balconies serve to increase the sense of space inside a home.
La cloison de verre ou de bois des patios arrière ou des balcons est une façon de gagner de l'espace dans la maison.
Wenn man Hinterhöfe oder Balkons mit Glas schließt, gewinnt man mehr Wohnraum.

157 Long, fixed windows in a corridor or the top part of a room are ideal for enhancing the penetration of natural light.
Les fenêtres en longueur à vitre fixe sont idéales pour favoriser l'entrée de lumière naturelle, dans le couloir ou à l'étage d'une pièce.
Damit mehr Tageslicht in den Raum fällt, kann man im Flur oder im oberen Teil des Raumes feste, längliche Glasfenster anbringen.

158 Window grids tend to make the opening look smaller, so it is best to replace them with a whole pane.
Les carreaux ayant tendance à réduire visuellement la taille de la fenêtre, il est judicieux de les remplacer par une vitre entière.
Quadratische Unterteilungen lassen das Fenster optisch kleiner wirken, deshalb sollte man möglichst einheitliche Glasflächen wählen.

159 Windows in thick walls create deep recesses that can be exploited to create benches by adding square, quilted cushions.
Les fenêtres dans les grands murs façonnent des alcôves profondes que l'on peut utiliser pour créer des bancs avec des coussins carrés et capitonnés.
Fenster in dicken Mauern lassen eine tiefe Öffnung entstehen, in denen man Bänke mit quadratischen Steppkissen unterbringen kann.

160 Corner windows broaden the visual perspective by extending interior spaces beyond their physical limits.
Les fenêtres d'angle agrandissent la perspective visuelle, ouvrant les espaces au-delà de leurs limites physiques.
Eckfenster erweitern die Perspektive und die Räume scheinen über ihre physischen Begrenzungen hinauszureichen.

© Laurent Brandaj

© Gnosis Architettura

© Laurent Brandajs

© Andrea Martiradonna

© Luuk Kramer

161 Spiral metal staircases are ideal for very small spaces.
Les escaliers métalliques en colimaçon sont idéals pour les espaces très réduits.
Wendeltreppen aus Metall eignen sich gut für kleine Räume.

162 Straight staircases do not take up much more room than spiral ones and they can have closets and chests of drawers fitted underneath them.
Les escaliers droits ne prennent pas beaucoup plus de place que ceux en colimaçon et permettent d'installer en dessous, placards et tiroirs.
Gerade verlaufende Treppen brauchen nicht viel mehr Platz als Wendeltreppen, und man kann unter ihnen Schränke und Schubladen anbringen.

163 If a staircase is set against a wall, the space underneath can be used as a small office area with a desk, computer and metal shelves.
Coller l'escalier au mur permet d'optimiser l'espace inférieur et d'y installer un mini bureau, avec table, ordinateur et étagère métallique.
Wenn die Treppe sich direkt an der Wand befindet, kann man den Raum unter der Treppe nutzen, um ein kleines Büro mit einem Tisch, einem Computer und einem Metallregal einzurichten.

164 Projecting metal steps lighten up the appearance of a staircase and do not cut off the view of the rest of the space.
Les marches flottantes en métal rendent l'escalier plus léger et n'obstruent pas la perspective visuelle du reste de la pièce.

© Ángel Baltaná

Frei schwebende Treppenstufen aus Metall lassen die Treppe leichter wirken und den Blick auf den übrigen Raum frei.

5 Glass or metacrylate banisters increase the sense of spaciousness because they do not form a visual obstacle.
Les rampes en verre ou méthacryliques donnent la sensation d'espace car elles dégagent la vue.
Treppengeländer aus Glas oder Metacrylat lassen den Raum größer wirken, weil es kein visuelles Hindernis gibt.

6 Staircases with just a few steps do not need banisters. If they are covered with the same material as the floor and the walls, they blend into their surroundings and do not appear to occupy any space.
Les escaliers avec peu de marches n'ont pas besoin de rampe. Revêtus du même matériau que celui du sol et des murs, ils se fondent dans l'ambiance et n'encombrent pas l'espace.
Treppen mit nur wenig Stufen benötigen keine Geländer. Wenn sie mit dem gleichen Material wie der Boden und die Wände verkleidet werden, fügen sie sich in die Umgebung ein und scheinen keinen Platz zu beanspruchen.

7 If steps are doubled in width and set into a small partition, the rear section can be used as bookshelves.
Doubler la taille des marches et incorporer à chacune d'elle une petite cloison, pour utiliser la partie arrière et y déposer des livres.
Wenn man die Größe der Stufen verdoppelt und in jeder davon eine kleine Trennwand anbringt, kann man den hinteren Teil als Bücherregal verwenden.

168 Landings can be fitted with magazine racks or thin shelves for holding CDs.
Les paliers peuvent abriter des étagères étroites pour ranger les CD ou des porte-revues suspendus.
In den Treppenabsätzen kann man kleine Regale für CDs oder hängende Zeitschriftenhalter anbringen.

169 Retractable staircases are ideal for small houses with a loft or a storage area in high ceilings.
Les escaliers escamotables sont parfaits pour les petites maisons avec grenier ou espaces de rangement dans les hauts plafonds.
Einziehbare Treppen eignen sich ausgezeichnet für kleine Wohnungen mit Mansarden oder Lagerbereiche in hohen Decken.

170 Short staircases spanning a small change in level can contain a hollow interior space; this can be reached by lifting the adjoining steps on hinges.
Les escaliers courts entre deux niveaux permettent d'avoir un espace intérieur creux auquel on peut accéder en relevant les marches avec un système de charnières.
Kurze Treppen, die verschiedene Ebenen miteinander verbinden, haben einen hohlen Innenraum, auf den man zugreifen kann, in dem man die Stufen hochhebt, die mit Scharnieren angebracht sind.

© Stefan Meyer

© Ángel Baltanás

© Joan Munc

© Luis Hevia

171 Platforms not only establish a hierarchy within various spaces but also provide storage possibilities.
Outre le fait de diviser les pièces en plusieurs espaces, les estrades créent également des zones de rangement.
Plattformen stellen nicht nur eine interessante Raumaufteilung dar, sondern sie bieten auch Lagerraum.

172 Boards made with medium-density fiber can be used in small, single-space apartments to divide them into four areas, two up and two down: kitchen, bedroom, dining room and closets.
Grâce à des panneaux de fibre de verre de densité moyenne, on peut diviser les petits appartements d'un seul espace de vie en quatre zones, deux en haut et deux en bas (cuisine, chambre, salle à manger et armoires).
Mittels MDF-Platten kann man kleine Wohnungen mit nur einem Raum in vier Bereiche untergliedern, zwei obere und zwei untere (Küche, Schlafzimmer, Esszimmer und Schränke).

173 A mezzanine that juts halfway across an apartment's surface area provides enough space for a bedroom and closets on the upper level.
Une mezzanine à mi-hauteur du volume total de l'appartement génère de l'espace pour la chambre à coucher et les armoires, au niveau supérieur.
Ein Zwischengeschoss, das die Hälfte der Gesamtfläche der Wohnung einnimmt, schafft Platz für ein Schlafzimmer und Schränke auf der oberen Ebene.

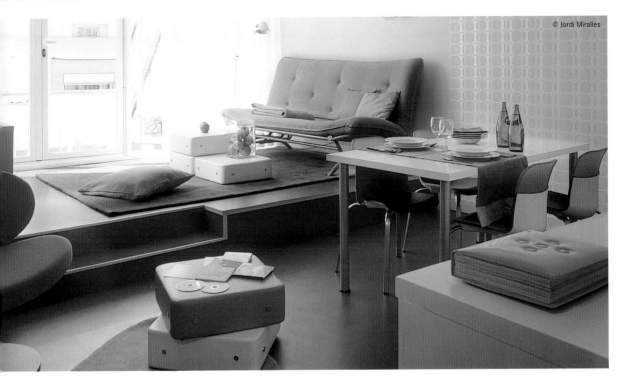

© Jordi Miralles

A platform in the form of a large box 6 feet high can contain a kitchen underneath and, above, a couch and central table that configure a living area.
Une estrade sous forme de grande boîte de deux mètres de haut, peut accueillir la cuisine : au dessus, un divan et une table basse pour former un salon.
Ein Podium, das wie eine große, zwei Meter hohe Kiste aussieht, nimmt unten eine Küche und oben ein Sofa und einen Couchtisch auf, um so ein Wohnzimmer entstehen zu lassen.

Even a narrow elevated walkway can fit in an office area.
Malgré leur étroitesse, les passerelles en hauteur peuvent accueillir un coin bureau.
Erhöhte schmale Laufstege können als Raum für das Büro dienen.

Metal mezzanines have the advantage of allowing light to pass from one floor to another.
Les mezzanines métalliques ont l'avantage de laisser circuler la lumière entre les différents étages.
Zwischengeschosse aus Metall haben den Vorteil, dass das Licht von einer Ebene in die nächste fällt.

If a bathtub or shower is set on a platform, the variation in height makes the bathroom look bigger.
Placer la baignoire ou la douche sur une estrade permet de créer différents niveaux qui agrandissent la salle de bains.

Wenn man die Badewanne oder die Dusche auf einem Podium installiert, wirkt das Bad durch den Höhenunterschied größer.

178 High beds are completely inappropriate in a bedroom installed on a platform in a loft-style home.
Les chambres à coucher installées sur une mezzanine dans les lofts ne peuvent pas accueillir de lit élevé.
In Schlafzimmern auf einem Podium in Loftwohnungen dürfen die Betten nicht hoch sein.

179 When houses have very low ceilings, the floor can be dug up to achieve the height required for a mezzanine.
Dans les maisons aux plafonds très bas, il est possible de creuser le sol jusqu'à obtenir la hauteur nécessaire pour créer une mezzanine.
Wenn die Decken in einem Haus sehr niedrig sind, kann man den Boden ausheben, um ein Zwischengeschoss zu schaffen.

180 When a mezzanine cuts across windows, blinds can be divided horizontally to create independent openings.
Si la mezzanine divise les fenêtres en deux, on peut couper les volets à l'horizontale pour créer des ouvertures indépendantes.
Wenn das Zwischengeschoss die Fenster unterbricht, können die Jalousien horizontal abgeschnitten werden, um unabhängige Öffnungen zu schaffen.

181 Beams constitute a structural element that gives a setting character.
space can be enlarged by eliminating the false ceilings that hide bear
Les poutres sont un élément structurel qui donne du caractère aux
espaces de vie. Eliminer les faux plafonds qui les masquent, permet
d'agrandir l'espace.
Träger sind Strukturelemente, die einem Raum einen eigenen Charakt
verleihen. Wenn man falsche Decken entfernt, welche die Dachbalker
verbergen, wirkt der Raum größer.

182 Wooden beams can be left exposed and untreated to give a space a
rustic touch.
On peut donner un côté rustique à l'espace de vie en laissant les
poutres en bois naturel apparentes.
Wenn man die Dachbalken sichtbar lässt und das Holz nicht streicht,
entsteht eine rustikale Wohnumgebung.

183 If the wooden beams in a ceiling are painted white and then given a
patina of gray, they become less eye-catching.
Peindre les poutres de bois du plafond en blanc et leur appliquer une
patine grise, leur confère une légèreté visuelle.
Wenn man die Dachbalken weiß streicht und eine graue Patina darübe
gibt, wirken sie leichter.

184 To maintain a contemporary look, it is best not to paint concrete bear
in settings that are covered with this material.

© Luis Hev

Pour garder le côté avant-gardiste, éviter de recouvrir les poutres avec du ciment, dans les pièces où ce matériau a été utilisé comme revêtement.

Um Räume, die mit Zement verkleidet sind, avantgardistisch wirken zu lassen, sollte man die Träger aus Zement nicht streichen.

5 The space between two vertical beams can be exploited by putting in one or two unobtrusive shelves.

L'espace entre deux poutres peut servir à placer une ou deux étagères légères.

Der Raum zwischen vertikalen Trägern kann für leichte Regale genutzt werden.

6 Transversal ceiling beams are ideal for installing rows of lights.

Les poutres de plafond transversales sont idéales pour installer des rails de spots de lumières.

Deckenbalken, die den Raum durchqueren, eignen sich ideal, um daran Lichtlinien anzubringen.

7 Beams painted black, or made of very dark wood, set an austere tone in a minimalist setting.

Les poutres peintes en noir, ou laissées en bois naturel, confèrent un air de sobriété aux ambiances minimalistes.

Schwarz gestrichene Balken oder Balken aus schwarzem Holz sind eine schlichte Lösung für minimalistische Wohnumgebungen.

188 Metal beams supporting glass ceilings are ideal for holding small plant pots and creating a small hanging garden.

Les poutres minimalistes qui soutiennent les plafonds de verre sont idéales pour y poser des petits pots de fleurs et créer un petit jardin suspendu.

Metallträger, die eine Glasdecke halten, eignen sich ideal für kleine Töpfe mit Pflanzen. So entsteht ein kleines, hängendes Gewächshaus.

189 In houses that are high and very narrow, the beams can be used to support an open attic space that can be used as an office.

Dans les maisons très étroites et en hauteur, les poutres permettent d'installer un demi étage pour y loger une mansarde ou un coin bureau.

In sehr schmalen und hohen Häusern kann man zwischen den Trägern ein Zwischengeschoss für eine Mansarde oder ein kleines Büro einziehen.

190 Although beams are attractive decorative elements, in very small spaces it is advisable to plaster them and then paint them the same color as the ceiling and walls.

Malgré leur atout décoratif, dans les espaces très petits, revêtir de préférence les poutres de plâtre et les peindre de la même couleur que le plafond et les murs.

Obwohl Balken ein schönes Dekorationselement sind, sollte man sie in sehr kleinen Räumen mit Gips verkleiden und in der gleichen Farbe wie die Decke und die Wände streichen.

© Stefan Meyer

© Paul O

© Paul Ott

191 Pillars are a good option in houses where a partition needs to be eliminated to gain space.

Les piliers sont utiles dans les maisons où il est nécessaire d'éliminer une cloison pour gagner de l'espace.

Säulen sind eine Lösung für Wohnungen, in denen man eine Trennwand beseitigt hat, um Platz zu gewinnen.

192 To emphasize the presence of pillars, paint them in a different color from the walls, to match the furniture.

Pour les mettre en évidence, les peindre dans une couleur différente des murs en harmonie avec le mobilier.

Um Säulen visuell zu betonen, sollten sie sich farblich von den Wänden unterscheiden, aber zu den Möbeln passen.

193 It is advisable to paint them white in loft-style homes, to avoid disrupting the space.

Pour ne pas entraver la sensation d'espace dans les maisons type loft, peindre de préférence les colonnes en blanc.

Um zu vermeiden, dass Säulen Wohnungen im Loftstil kleiner wirken lassen, sollte man sie weiß streichen.

194 Polished aluminum pillars reflect the surrounding environment and tend to be visually unobtrusive.

Les colonnes en aluminium poli reflètent l'ambiance alentour et tendent à s'effacer visuellement.

© Gregory Goode

Säulen aus glänzendem Aluminium spiegeln die Umgebung wider und verschmelzen mit ihr.

5 If a setting is dominated by concrete, vertical beams clad in this material give a unifying effect.

Là où le béton est omniprésent, il est conseillé de recouvrir les poutres verticales d'un coffrage dans ce matériau pour unifier l'espace.

Wenn in einer Wohnung Beton als Material vorherrscht, lassen vertikale, mit Aluminium umhüllte Träger den Raum einheitlicher wirken.

6 A space can be enlivened by rustic wooden pillars painted white with a patina of gray.

Les colonnes en bois rustique, peintes en blanc avec une pointe de patine grise, allègent les espaces.

Weiß gestrichene Säulen aus rustikalem Holz mit einer Patina in Grau lassen den Raum leichter wirken.

7 A screen placed between two pillars serves as a partition that can be easily removed.

Un paravent placé entre deux piliers joue le rôle de cloison facilement amovible.

Ein Wandschirm zwischen zwei Säulen dient als Trennwand, die leicht entfernt werden kann.

8 If a space is very small, it is not a good idea to hang pictures on a pillar as this prevents the latter from blending into its surroundings.

Dans un très petit espace de vie, éviter d'utiliser le pilier pour accrocher des tableaux ou photos qui l'empêcheraient de se fondre à l'environnement.

Wenn der Raum sehr klein ist, sollte man an den Säulen keine Gemälde oder Fotos aufhängen, weil sie sich sonst zu stark von ihrer Umgebung abheben.

199 When pillars are very close to a wall, the space in between can be exploited to install shelves or a low piece of furniture that allows light to pass through.

Quand les piliers sont très proches des murs, l'espace intermédiaire peut être utilisé pour installer des étagères ou un meuble bas qui laisse passer la lumière.

Wenn die Säulen sehr nah an den Wänden stehen, kann der Platz dazwischen für ein Regal oder ein niedriges Möbel genutzt werden, das Licht durchlässt.

200 The space between two pillars can be used to hang a hammock, as an informal alternative to a couch.

Profiter de l'espace entre deux piliers pour accrocher un hamac : une solution plus informelle que le divan.

Der Raum zwischen zwei Säulen kann für eine Hängematte genutzt werden; eine unkonventionelle Alternative zu einem Sofa.

© Yael Pincus

© Yael Pincus

© Paul Ott

201 The more dividing panels that are knocked down, the greater the resulting sense of spaciousness.

Pour agrandir l'espace, il faut intégrer les zones de vie en éliminant les cloisons.

Je mehr Peneele entfernt werden, desto Grösser wird der Gewonnene Raum.

202 Glass panels offer an excellent way of dividing areas without reducing their size.

Pour garder cette notion de grand espace de vie, tout en le divisant, les cloisons de verre sont idéales.

Um weiter Räume mit Aufteilungen zu schaffen, eignen sich Glaspanee ausgezeichnet.

203 The latest trends in decoration have revived screens, albeit in compact formats and covered with wallpaper or a large black-and-white photo.

Dans la décoration intérieure, les dernières tendances remettent les paravents au goût du jour, mais en petit format, compacts et habillés d papiers peints ou d'une photo format poster en noir et blanc.

Der neuste Trend in der Raumgestaltung hat die spanische Wand wiede neu aufleben lassen, aber in kompakter Form, mit Tapeten oder einem großen Ausdruck eines Schwarzweißfotos verkleidet.

204 Wooden walls that turn into sliding doors offer a good way of separating a bedroom from a sitting room.

© Bjorg Arnasdottir

Les murs lambrissés qui se transforment en portes coulissantes sont une solution judicieuse pour séparer la chambre à coucher du salon.
Holzwände, die zur Schiebetür werden, sind eine gute Lösung, um das Schlafzimmer vom Wohnzimmer zu trennen.

5 Panels made of glass bricks have the advantage of dividing a space without blocking the entrance of light.
Les cloisons en briques de verre offrent l'avantage de diviser l'espace de vie sans empêcher la lumière de circuler.
Paneele aus Glasbausteinen haben den Vorteil, den Raum zu unterteilen, ohne das Licht abzublocken.

6 Colored S-shape metacrylate screens are ideal for separating a kitchen from the rest of the house.
Les panneaux en méthacrylate de couleur en forme de S sont idéals pour séparer la cuisine du reste de la maison.
Durchsichtige Türen aus Metacrylat in S-Form sind ideal, um die Küche vom übrigen Raum abzutrennen.

7 When a bed is set under a staircase, a medium-height panel covered with fabric at the level of the headboard not only serves as a partition but also creates storage space.
Lorsque le lit est placé sous un escalier, un panneau tapissé à mi-hauteur en guise de tête de lit sert de cloison séparatrice et crée un espace de rangement.

Wenn sich das Bett unter einer Treppe befindet, dient ein mittelhohes, mit Stoff verkleidetes Paneel am Kopfteil als Raumteiler und es entsteht ein Lagerraum.

208 Accordion-style wooden panels are ideal for separating built-in kitchens from the rest of the home.
Les cloisons en bois en accordéon sont idéales pour séparer les cuisines américaines du reste de la maison.
Falttüren eignen sich ideal, um offene Küchen vom Rest der Wohnung abzutrennen.

209 The plastic algae designed by the Bouroullec brothers can be grouped together to form a thin, translucent dividing panel.
Les algues en plastique dont le design porte la signature des frères Bouroullec peuvent s'assembler pour former une fine cloison translucide.
Die von den Brüdern Bouroullec entworfenen Kunststoffalgen können so miteinander verbunden werden, dass ein dünnes, lichtdurchlässiges, raumteilendes Paneel entsteht.

210 Modular panels with a textured surface or relief can be used to organize a setting.
Les cloisons modulaires au revêtement en relief ou texturé distribuent les différents espaces.
Modulare Paneele mit Oberflächen mit Relief oder Textur dienen als Trennelemente für verschiedene Wohnbereiche.

© Matteo Piazza

© Matteo Piazza

© Matteo Piazza

© Satoshi Okada Architects

© Matteo Piazz

211 Doors tend to go unnoticed if they are in natural wood or are painted the same color as the rest of the space.

Les portes en bois naturel ou peintes de la même couleur que le reste de l'espace ambiant passent en général inaperçues.

Türen aus Naturholz oder Türen, die in der gleichen Farbe wie der übrig Raum gestrichen sind, verschmelzen mit ihrer Umgebung.

212 It is not advisable to paint a frame a different color from the door in small spaces; this makes the walls look smaller.

Dans les petits univers, éviter de peindre l'encadrement de la porte d'une couleur différente de celle-ci, car cela rapetisse les murs.

In kleinen Räumen sollte man den Türrahmen nicht in einer anderen Farbe als die der Tür streichen, weil dies die Wände optisch verkleinert

213 Sliding doors are an excellent device for saving space, as long as sufficient wall space is available.

Tant que la surface du mur le permet, les portes coulissantes sont idéales pour gagner de l'espace.

Wenn an der Wand genug Platz ist, sind Schiebetüren die ideale Lösung um Platz zu sparen.

214 Doors with acid-treated glass panes allow light to pass through a space They are more visually appealing if they are fitted into an ash frame.

Les portes en plaques de verre traitées à l'acide laissent circuler la lumière dans tout l'espace. Les chambranles en bois de hêtre leur confèrent une chaleur visuelle.

© Nuria Fuentes

© Satoshi Okada Architects

Türen aus geätztem Glas lassen Licht in die verschiedenen Bereiche fallen. Mit einem Rahmen aus Buchenholz wirken sie weniger kalt.

Zum Aufhängen von Mützen, Schals, Ketten und Gürteln gibt es spezielle Kleiderhaken in Form einer Stange, die man an die Tür hängt und die unsichtbar bleiben, solange die Tür geöffnet ist.

5   In extremely modern settings, it is possible to cover doors with the same wallpaper as the doors of a room. This enhances the sense of spaciousness and creates a surprising effect.
Les univers plus modernes affichent des portes habillées du même papier peint que les murs de la pièce. Le gain d'espace ainsi obtenu est accompagné d'un effet de surprise.
In modern gestalteten Wohnungen kann man die Türen mit der gleichen Tapete wie die Wände verkleiden. So wird Platz gewonnen und ein interessanter Effekt geschaffen.

6   Doors with wooden slats (similar to blinds) also induce a sense of spaciousness.
Les portes recouvertes de lattes de bois à la manière de persienne créent également une sensation d'espace.
Türen mit Holzjalousien lassen den Raum ebenfalls größer wirken.

7   Special hangers in the form of a bar attached to a door are now available for storing hats, scarves, belts and dog collars. The bar is not visible when the door is open.
Pour accrocher bonnets, écharpes, colliers ou ceintures, il existe des portemanteaux spéciaux composés d'une barre qui s'accroche aux portes et reste masquée lorsque la porte est ouverte.

218   Wherever possible, it is best to eliminate doors that divide continuous spaces.
Autant que faire se peut, choisir d'éliminer les portes entre des espaces contigus.
Immer, wenn dies möglich ist, sollte man trennende Türen zwischen aufeinander folgenden Räumen entfernen.

219   Very high doors tend to make spaces look narrower. Their height can be reduced by using the space above the upper part of the frame for shelves.
Les portes très hautes tendent à rétrécir l'espace. En réduire la hauteur est facile. Pour ce faire, utiliser l'espace du cadre supérieur comme étagère.
Sehr hohe Türen lassen den Raum enger wirken. Man kann sie niedriger machen, indem man den Teil des Rahmens als Regal benutzt.

220   A door covered with a single sheet of wood (rather than strips) is a perfect match for uncluttered spaces.
Les portes habillées de bois d'un seul tenant (au lieu de listels de bois) se marient bien avec les espaces sobres.
Türen, die mit einer einzigen Holzplatte (statt mit Holzlatten) verkleidet sind, passen gut in klar strukturierte Räume.

© Trevor Ma

© Joan Roig

221 Replacing a dividing wall with a large, fixed blind made of natural wood provides a way of gaining both space and luminosity.
Remplacer un grand mur de partition par une grande persienne fixe en bois naturel offre un gain d'espace et de luminosité.
Wenn man eine Trennwand durch eine große, feste Jalousie aus Naturholz ersetzt, gewinnt man mehr Licht und scheinbar mehr Raum.

222 Blinds hanging from a wall are ideal for separating an office area from the rest of a sitting room.
Les persiennes accrochées au mur sont idéales pour séparer la zone du bureau du reste du salon.
Jalousien, die an der Wand hängen, eignen sich ideal, um das Büro vom Rest des Wohnzimmers abzutrennen.

223 An Oriental look is enhanced by the use of pleated blinds in natural fibers or material resembling paper.
Pour accentuer le caractère oriental de certains espaces, utiliser des persiennes plissées en fibres naturelles ou en simili papier.
Bei in orientalischem Stil dekorierten Wohnungen wird die Wirkung noch verstärkt, wenn man gefaltete Jalousien aus Naturfasern oder papierähnliche Rollos verwendet.

224 The addition of bamboo blinds adds warmth to settings dominated by white.
Recourir aux persiennes de bambou permet de créer une note chaleureuse dans les espaces dominés par le blanc.

© Murray Fredericks

Um Wohnungen, in denen Weiß dominiert, wärmer wirken zu lassen, kann man Bambusjalousien aufhängen.

5   In the case of windows occupying an entire wall, vertical blinds are elegant and more formal than horizontal ones.
Pour les verrières qui occupent tout un pan de mur, les persiennes verticales sont une solution élégante, moins informelle que les horizontales.
Bei Vitrinen, die eine ganze Wand einnehmen, stellen vertikale Jalousien eine elegante Lösung dar; sie sind unkonventioneller als horizontale.

6   Cotton or linen blinds have the advantage of allowing light to filter through diffusely even when they are drawn.
Les persiennes en coton ou lin offrent l'avantage de diffuser la lumière même une fois fermées.
Jalousien aus Baumwolle oder Leinen lassen sogar im geschlossenen Zustand noch ein diffuses Licht durch.

7   Roller blinds can be fitted to the exact size of the window. Their extremely thin rods allow the entrance of light to be regulated to the extent of achieving a complete blackout.
Les persiennes unicellulaires s'adaptent à la taille exacte de la fenêtre. Leurs baguettes très fines permettent de régler l'arrivée de lumière jusqu'à obtention d'un effet de *black out* total.
Einteilige Jalousien passen sich genau an die Fenstergröße an. Ihre Stäbchen sind sehr klein und schmal, so dass man das Licht

ausgezeichnet regulieren kann. Ganz geschlossen herrscht im Raum absolute Dunkelheit.

228   White roller blinds make windows look bigger.
Les persiennes enroulables, blanches, agrandissent visuellement les ouvertures.
Weiße Rollos vergrößern die Fenster optisch.

229   Metal blinds go well with stone or polished concrete covering in bathrooms with clean-cut lines.
Dans les salles de bain aux lignes épurées, les persiennes version métal se marient à merveille aux revêtements de pierre ou de ciment poli et ciré.
Metalljalousien passen gut zu Bädern mit klaren Linien, die mit Naturstein oder Zementglattstrich verkleidet sind.

230   In order to enhance the sensation of spaciousness, blinds can be extended past a window down to the floor.
Pour accroître la sensation d'espace, les persiennes peuvent descendre jusqu'au sol et même dépasser la taille de la fenêtre.
Um den Raum optisch größer wirken zu lassen, sollten die Jalousien bis zum Boden reichen und sogar größer als die Fenster sein.

© Alejandro Bahamón

© Rupert Steiner

231 The drapes in small spaces should be in neutral colors with unobtrusive designs.
Dans les petits espaces, choisir des rideaux aux imprimés délicats et couleurs neutres.
In kleinen Räumen sollte man Gardinen mit feinen Drucken und neutralen Farben wählen.

232 Heavy materials like velvet and brocades can be overpowering.
Les matières lourdes, comme le velours ou les brocarts, alourdissent trop l'espace.
Schwere Materialien wie Samt oder Brokat lassen die Dekoration schnell überladen wirken.

233 Drapes should be in the same color as the other furnishings or, in a room that is predominantly white, stand out as the only splash of color.
La couleur des rideaux doit s'accorder au reste du mobilier, ou alors, dans une pièce où le blanc prédomine, ils doivent être l'unique élément coloré de contraste.
Die Farben der Gardinen sollten zu den übrigen Möbeln passen. Falls in einem Raum die Farbe Weiß dominiert, können die Gardinen als einziges farbiges Element einen Kontrast bilden.

234 Lacy drapes have come back into fashion, used on their own to provide luminosity while guaranteeing privacy.
Les voilages d'un seul tenant sont à la mode parce qu'ils apportent la lumière sans nuire à l'intimité.

© Hisao Suzu

Gardinen vor den Scheiben liegen im Trend, und zwar als einziges dekoratives Element. Sie lassen Licht einfallen, schützen jedoch vor unerwünschten Einblicken.

Heavy drapes in white, ivory or pale gray serve to separate spaces. Pockets can also be sewn into them for storage purposes.
Les rideaux en tissu lourd et blanc, ivoire ou gris clair servent à séparer les zones de vie. En outre, on peut les agrémenter de petites poches cousues, utiles pour le rangement.
Gardinen aus schwerem Stoff in Weiß, Elfenbein oder Hellgrau dienen zum Abteilen verschiedener Bereiche. Außerdem kann man Taschen einnähen, in denen man Objekte aufbewahrt.

Thin steel bars help to reduce the visual impact of drapes.
Les barres fines en métal couleur acier allègent visuellement les rideaux.
Feine Stangen aus stahlfarbenem Metall lassen die Gardinen optisch leichter wirken.

The latest trend is to bring back drapes made of thin metal threads as a means of partially dividing spaces.
Pour séparer partiellement les sphères de vie, le dernier cri est d'utiliser des rideaux au fin maillage de métal.
Der neuste Trend zum teilweisen Abtrennen von Wohnbereichen sind Gardinen aus feinen Metallfäden.

238 Drapes made of colored glass beads add a naive touch and reflect light at the end of a corridor or in any indoor opening.
Les rideaux de boules de verre colorées, à l'entrée du couloir ou sur toute autre ouverture intérieure, apportent une touche naïve et reflètent la lumière.
Perlengardinen aus Glaskugeln am Eingang des Flurs oder an Türen im Inneren wirken frisch und verspielt und reflektieren das Licht.

239 Floral designs and other motifs can be overwhelming, so they should only be used against pale backgrounds.
Les imprimés à fleurs ou autres motifs alourdissent l'espace. Ils ne tolèrent que des fonds clairs.
Blumendrucke und andere Motive wirken überladen und sollten nur gewählt werden, wenn der Hintergrund hell ist.

240 Drapes that run from the ceiling to the floor make a room look bigger.
Les rideaux allant du sol au plafond agrandissent les pièces.
Gardinen, die von der Decke bis zum Boden reichen, lassen den Raum größer wirken.

© Paul Ott

© Trevor Ma

© Matteo Piazza

241 When a dining room and living area share the same space, low furnitu
can separate the two settings without cramping them.
Lorsque la salle à manger et le salon partagent un même espace, les
meubles bas peuvent séparer les deux univers sans pour autant
entraver l'ampleur visuelle.
Wenn sich das Ess- und das Wohnzimmer im gleichen Raum befinden,
kann man beide Bereiche mit niedrigen Möbeln voneinander abtrenne
ohne visuell an Weite zu verlieren.

242 Bookcases with no rear panel can divide spaces while still allowing lig
to pass through.
Les bibliothèques sans fond séparent les univers tout en laissant filtre
la lumière.
Bücherregale ohne Hinterwand unterteilen Bereiche, lassen aber Licht
durch.

243 In a home revolving around a corridor with the bathroom and kitchen i
adjacent spaces, the same worktop can be used to install two separat
sinks.
Dans une maison organisée en couloir, où la salle de bains et la cuisin
sont contiguës, on peut utiliser le même plan de travail pour les deux.
In einer Wohnung, welche die Form eines langen Ganges hat, in der
Küche und Bad aneinander grenzen, kann man die gleiche Installation
für das Waschbecken und für das Spülbecken benutzen.

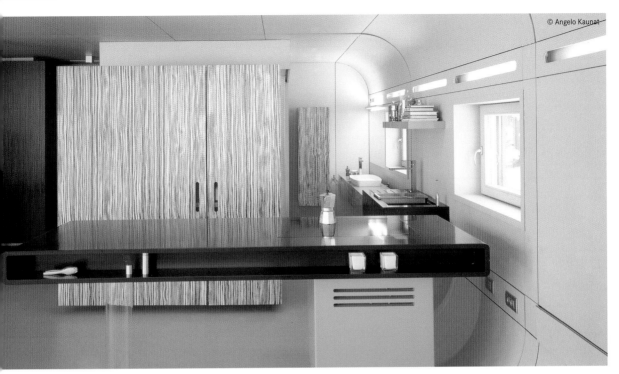

© Angelo Kaunat

Modular structures that make it possible to replace a shelf with a table top are ideal for single-space homes with a built-in kitchen.

Les structures modulaires permettant de remplacer une étagère par une table sont idéales pour les maisons à espace de vie unique doté d'une cuisine américaine.

Modulare Strukturen, bei denen ein Regal durch einen Tisch ersetzt werden kann, eignen sich ausgezeichnet für Wohnungen mit nur einem Raum und offener Küche.

When a bedroom is separated from a living area by a closet, it is advisable to paper its back side to make it look like a panel.

Lorsqu'une armoire sépare la chambre à coucher du salon, tapisser la partie arrière du meuble pour qu'elle s'assimile à une cloison.

Wenn ein Schrank das Schlafzimmer vom Wohnbereich abtrennt, kann man die Rückwand des Schrankes tapezieren, so dass sie wie eine Wand wirkt.

Low chests of drawers or shelf units with rollers are ideal for separating settings with several uses.

Les commodes ou étagères basses sur roulettes sont idéales pour séparer les espaces polyvalents.

Niedrige Kommoden oder Regale mit Rädern eignen sich ausgezeichnet, um Bereiche voneinander abzutrennen, die mehreren Wohnfunktionen dienen.

247 Placing high benches around the console separating a built-in kitchen from a sitting room creates a small dining area.

Placer des tabourets autour de la crédence qui sépare la cuisine américaine du salon, permet de créer une petite salle à manger.

Wenn man um die Konsole, welche die offene Küche vom Wohnzimmer trennt, hohe Bänke montiert, entsteht ein kleiner Essbereich.

248 A couch set with its back to the dining room table separates this area from the sitting room.

Un divan adossé à la table de la salle à manger, la sépare du salon.

Ein Sofa hinter dem Esstisch trennt den Essbereich vom Wohnbereich.

249 A clothes rack with a support serves as a mobile divider in homes with little furniture and modern decoration.

Un portemanteau à coulisse sur un support fait office de cloison amovible dans les maisons peu meublées et à décoration contemporaine.

Eine Kleiderstange mit Führung dient als bewegliches Trennelement in Wohnungen mit wenig Möbeln und moderner Dekoration.

250 One or two hanging (or 'bubble') chairs help to define a setting without occupying too much space.

Un ou deux sièges suspendus (connus sous le nom de *bubble chairs*) permettent de définir une sphère de vie sans remplir l'espace.

Ein oder zwei hängende Kugelsessel, auch bubble chairs genannt, definieren die Bereiche, ohne viel Platz wegzunehmen.

Lighting
Éclairage
Beleuchtung

Light can mold a room by redefining its physical limits and creating spaces that could not exist otherwise. Effective lighting allows small homes to benefit from some of the luxuries associated with larger houses, such as wallpaper, brick and dark leather furniture. A good combination of light sources on the floor, walls and ceilings makes a home inviting without forsaking any practical considerations.

La lumière façonne les pièces, redéfinit leurs limites physiques et crée des espaces qui ne pourraient exister autrement. Un bon éclairage permet aux petites maisons de s'offrir des petits luxes liés aux grands espaces, à l'instar des papiers peints, de la brique ou du mobilier en cuir foncé. Une bonne association de sources de lumière au niveau du sol, des murs et des plafonds transforme la maison en un espace accueillant, sans nuire à la fonctionnalité.

Licht gestaltet den Raum, definiert die physischen Grenzen neu und schafft Umgebungen, die sonst nicht existieren könnten. Mit einer guten Beleuchtung kann man in kleinen Häusern Dekorationen und Materialen benutzen, die sonst nur in große Häuser passen, wie zum Beispiel Tapeten, Ziegelsteine und dunkle Ledermöbel. Eine gute Kombination der Lichtquellen auf Bodenhöhe, an den Wänden und Decken macht die Wohnung zu einem einladenden Ort, ohne dabei die Funktionalität aus den Augen zu verlieren.

© Adrián Gregorutti

© Eric Koyama

© B. Lux

© B. Lu

251 A hanging lamp should not be the main feature of a small living room. Lamps with a transparent metacrylate shade emit plenty of light and blend into the surroundings.

Dans un petit salon, les suspensions ne sont pas idéales. Les lampes avec abat-jour en méthacrylate transparent génèrent une lumière intense et se fondent à l'ambiance.

In einem kleinen Wohnzimmer darf eine Hängelampe nicht die Hauptrolle spielen. Lampen mit Schirmen aus transparentem Metacryl spenden viel Licht und gehen in ihrer Umgebung auf.

252 A single ceiling light produces lighting with strong contrasts. More appealing settings can be created by combining several sources of indirect light.

Un seul plafonnier produit un éclairage très contrasté. Avec un jeu de différents foyers de lumière indirecte, on obtient des ambiances plus accueillantes.

Eine einzige Deckenlampe lässt eine relativ harte Beleuchtung entstehen. Wenn man mit mehreren Scheinwerfern eine indirekte Beleuchtung schafft, wirkt die Wohnung gemütlicher.

253 Ceiling lights with hanging metal pieces are extremely reflective and produce rich textures.

Les plafonniers à pièces métalliques en suspension ont une grande capacité de réflexion et confèrent à la lumière une texture riche.

Deckenlampen mit hängenden Metallteilen sind sehr reflektierend und geben dem Licht eine reiche Textur.

© Amit Geron

The paler the colors on the walls and ceilings, the less light that is required. In these cases, a few strategically placed, flush-fitting lights on the walls are sufficient.

Plus les couleurs des murs et plafonds sont claires, moins il est nécessaire d'avoir une lumière forte. Dans ce cas, des appliques judicieusement réparties sur les murs sont suffisantes.

Je heller die Farben der Wand und der Decken sind, umso weniger Licht wird benötigt. In diesen Fällen genügen über die Wände verteilte Wandleuchten.

Corridors look bigger with a line of portholes running along the ceiling.

Une rangée d'oeils-de-boeuf le long du plafond permet d'agrandir les couloirs.

Flure wirken größer, wenn man eine Reihe von eingelassenen Strahlern an der Decke anbringt.

Rooms look bigger if their ceiling and walls are illuminated.

Avec un éclairage sur les murs et au plafond, les pièces semblent plus grandes.

Wenn man die Decke und die Wände beleuchtet, wirkt der Raum größer.

In single-space homes, the lamp in the dining area must be set three feet above the table to differentiate this setting from the rest of the room.

Dans les maisons à espace de vie unique, la lampe de la salle à manger doit être installée à un mètre de hauteur au-dessus de la table pour différencier cet espace du reste de la pièce.

In Wohnungen mit nur einem einzigen Raum sollte die Esszimmerlampe einen Meter über dem Tisch hängen, um den Essbereich von den übrigen Bereichen zu unterscheiden.

258 Wall lamps set alongside the bed add warmth to a bedroom more effectively than a ceiling light.

Pour rendre une chambre à coucher chaleureuse, les appliques sur les côtés du lit sont plus efficaces que les plafonniers.

Um ein Schlafzimmer warm und einladend wirken zu lassen, eignen sich Wandlampen neben dem Bett besser als eine Deckenlampe.

259 General lighting is optimized by the use of white lamps; it is advisable to reserve colored lamps for individual areas.

Les lampes blanches optimisent l'éclairage d'ensemble : celles qui dégagent une lumière colorée sont idéales pour un éclairage partiel.

Für die allgemeine Beleuchtung eignen sich Lampen mit weißem Licht besser. Farbige Lampen eignen sich nur für die Beleuchtung bestimmter Zonen.

260 Lighting rails on the ceiling do not take up any space and make it possible to focus spotlights as required.

Les rails de lumière au plafond ne prennent pas de place et permettent de diriger les spots sur les endroits à mettre en évidence.

Lichtschienen an der Decke nehmen keinen Platz weg und ermöglichen es, die Strahler in jede beliebige Richtung zu lenken.

© Juan Merine

© Murray Fredericks

© Matteo Piazza

© Satoshi Okada Architects

© B. Lux

© B. Lu

261 Movable ceiling lights that can be directly focused on to a wall are idea for picking out decorative elements like a picture or a mirror.

Pour mettre en valeur des éléments décoratifs, comme un tableau ou un miroir, les plafonniers orientables sont idéals, car ils peuvent être dirigés directement sur le mur.

Um dekorative Elemente wie ein Gemälde oder einen Spiegel hervorzuheben, eignen sich verstellbare Deckenleuchten gut, denn ma kann sie auch direkt auf die Wand richten.

262 Floor-level lighting makes a space look bigger. Metacrylate cubes illuminated from within can also serve as side tables.

La lumière au ras du sol agrandit l'espace. Les cubes en méthacrylate avec lumière intérieure servent également de tables d'appoint.

Licht auf Bodenhöhe lässt die Räumlichkeiten größer wirken. Würfel au Metacrylat, die von innen beleuchtet sind, dienen als Beistelltische.

263 Table lamps with very large shades and dark colors make small spaces look even tinier; in this case, lampshades with fringes or tulles are mor appropriate.

Les lampes de table avec de très grands abat-jour de couleur foncée ont tendance à rapetisser les espaces très petits : dans ce cas, préfére les lampes en caireles *ou tulle.*

Tischlampen mit großen Schirmen in dunklen Farben lassen kleine Räume optisch noch kleiner wirken. Besser eignen sich Lampen mit Glasverzierungen oder Tüll.

© B. Lux

© B. Lux

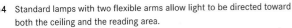

4 Standard lamps with two flexible arms allow light to be directed toward both the ceiling and the reading area.
Les lampadaires dotés de deux bras flexibles permettent d'orienter la lumière vers le plafond et vers la zone de lecture.
Stehlampen mit zwei beweglichen Armen machen es möglich, das Licht zur Decke und zum Lesebereich zu lenken.

5 A wooden bookcase can be lit by strings of spotlights set on each shelf.
Les rayonnages en bois peuvent être éclairés par des rangées de lampes au-dessus de chaque étagère.
Simse aus Holz kann man mit einer Reihe von Strahlern beleuchten, die sich in jedem Regal befinden.

6 Apart from general lighting, a bathroom needs wall lamps above the mirror and next to the shower.
En plus de l'éclairage d'ensemble, la salle de bains nécessite une applique sur le miroir et une autre à côté de la douche.
Zusätzlich zur allgemeinen Beleuchtung benötigt man im Bad eine Wandlampe über dem Spiegel und eine weitere neben der Dusche.

7 A table light in one part of the bedroom helps to create a more luminous setting by eliminating contrasts of light and shade.
Une lampe de table n'importe où dans la chambre à coucher permet de créer une ambiance plus diaphane en éliminant les contrastes d'ombre et de lumière.

Eine Tischlampe im Schlafzimmer sorgt für klareres Licht, weil starke Kontraste zwischen Licht und Schatten vermieden werden.

268 Wall lights positioned above the headboard are ideal for reading in bed.
Pour lire dans la chambre à coucher, les appliques murales installées au-dessus de la tête de lits sont idéales.
Um im Schlafzimmer lesen zu können, eignen sich Strahler an der Wand, die sich über dem Kopfteil des Bettes befinden.

269 Fluorescent tubes set underneath closets make a kitchen look bigger.
Les tubes fluorescents placés sous les placards de la cuisine agrandissent l'espace.
Leuchtstoffröhren unter den Küchenschränken lassen den Raum größer wirken.

270 When lighting is complemented by candles, a combination of various shapes and sizes is most effective, although their color should be uniform.
Pour compléter l'éclairage par des bougies, choisir un mélange de formes et tailles diverses, mais une seule couleur.
Wenn man die Beleuchtung durch Kerzen ergänzt, sieht eine Kombination verschiedener Formen und Größen in der gleichen Farbe sehr schön aus.

© Margherita Spilulli

© Joan Mundó

© Shania Shegedyn

© Joan Mundó

© Paul Ott

© Angelo Kauna

© Yael Pincus

271 Overhead light penetrating through windows in the ceiling tends to be dispersed throughout a house.

La lumière zénithale qui entre par les fenêtres de toit a tendance à se diffuser dans tous les espaces de la maison.

Licht von oben, das durch die Deckenfenster einfällt, erreicht meist alle Bereiche des Hauses.

272 When windows are not very large, it is advisable to add a layer of polished concrete or stone to the floor in order to reflect sunlight.

Si les fenêtres ne sont pas très grandes, opter pour un revêtement de sol en ciment ou béton ciré pour réfléchir la lumière naturelle.

Wenn die Fenster nicht sehr groß sind, sollte man für den Boden Zementglattstrich oder polierte Steine wählen, die das Tageslicht reflektieren.

273 Reflectors can be used to capture sunlight and direct it toward a first-floor patio.

Les réflecteurs qui captent la lumière du soleil peuvent la diriger vers les patios au rez-de-chaussée d'un bâtiment.

Reflektoren, die das Sonnenlicht auffangen, können dieses in die Räume des ersten Stocks eines Gebäudes lenken.

274 Solar tubes or conduits capable of carrying light for distances of over 30 feet are ideal for spaces in which it is impossible to install skylights.

© Hanse Haus

Les tubes ou conduits solaires qui transportent la lumière au-delà de 10 mètres sont idéals dans les espaces où il est impossible d'installer des lucarnes.

Rohre oder andere Leitungen für Sonnenlicht, die das Licht über 10 Meter weit transportieren, eignen sich ausgezeichnet für Räume, in denen man keine Dachfenster einbauen kann.

5 When an inner patio is closed off with a glass roof, it is a good idea to use glass for the walls as well.

Lorsque l'on couvre un patio à l'aide d'un toit de verre, employer le même matériau sur les murs.

Wenn man einen Innenhof mit einem Glasdach schließt, sollte man die Wände ebenfalls verglasen.

6 A small horizontal opening in the top part of a wall makes a room seem bigger.

Une petite rainure horizontale en haut du mur donne l'impression d'agrandir une pièce.

Ein kleiner horizontaler Schlitz am oberen Teil der Wand lässt den Raum optisch weiter wirken.

7 Mirrors set on walls opposite windows provide a very effective means of enhancing natural light.

Les miroirs accrochés à des murs opposés aux fenêtres sont efficaces pour optimaliser la lumière naturelle.

Spiegel, die den Fenstern gegenüber an den Wänden hängen, dienen zum Verstärken des Tageslichts.

278 High pieces of furniture block the entrance of sunlight, so it is best to place them against a wall in front of a window.

Les meubles en hauteur empêchent la lumière d'entrer. Les placer de préférence sur le mur opposé à la fenêtre.

Hohe Möbel behindern den Lichteinfall, deshalb ist es besser, sie dem Fenster gegenüber aufzustellen.

279 It is advisable to connect different settings by means of openings or arches if sunlight is required to penetrate into all of them.

Pour que la lumière naturelle circule à travers l'espace, relier les zones de vie par le biais d'ouvertures ou d'arcs.

Um Tageslicht in verschiedene Bereiche zu leiten, sollten diese durch Öffnungen oder Bögen miteinander verbunden sein.

280 An exterior view acquires added importance if windows are painted the same color as the walls and decorated with pale drapes.

Les fenêtres peintes de la même couleur que les murs et agrémentées de rideaux clairs accentuent le rôle de l'espace extérieur.

Wenn man die Fenster in der gleichen Farbe wie die Wände streicht und helle Gardinen benutzt, stellt man eine Beziehung nach draußen her.

Colors

Couleurs

Farben

The appearance of a home can be significantly altered by a particular approach to color. The application of color on walls, floors and ceilings modifies our perceived dimensions of rooms; similarly, its presence or absence on furniture and textiles helps to define spaces. Colors also affect the state of mind, so the choice of a specific color is a decisive factor in people's relationships with the space in which they live.

L'art et la manière d'utiliser une couleur peuvent modifier considérablement l'apparence d'un espace. Son application sur les murs, sols et plafonds modifie la dimension des pièces, alors que sa présence ou absence sur le mobilier et les tissus définissent les espaces. Elles ont également un effet psychologique sur l'état d'âme : il est donc primordial de choisir la couleur en fonction de la maison et de ses habitants.

Die Art und Weise, wie man die Farben einsetzt, kann eine Wohnung entscheidend verändern. Farben an den Wänden, Böden und Decken verändern scheinbar die Größe des Raums, und starke oder neutrale Farben der Möbel und Textilien definieren die Raumaufteilung. Auch der Gemützstand wird von den Farben beeinflusst. Deshalb ist es wichtig, die richtigen Farben für die Menschen zu wählen, welche die Wohnung bewohnen.

© Matteo Piazza

© Reto Guntli, Agi Simoes/Zapaimag

© Matteo Piazza

281 Spaces entirely painted in warm colors tend to look small, so it is important to leave one surface white.
Les espaces peints surtout dans des tons chauds tendent à paraître plus petits. Il est alors important de garder une surface blanche.
Räume, die nur in warmen Farben gestrichen sind, wirken optisch kleiner. In diesem Fall ist es wichtig, dass einige der Flächen weiß sind.

282 When combined with orange, yellow can serve the same function as white in creating an impression of spaciousness.
Le jaune associé à l'orange produit le même effet d'espace que le blanc.
Gelb in Kombination mit Orange erfüllt die gleiche Funktion wie Weiß, wenn es um die Empfindung der Raumgröße geht.

283 Bedrooms with wooden or dark brown furniture can be made brighter through the addition of fabrics in warm colors.
Les chambres à coucher dotées de meubles en bois ou de couleur chocolat gagnent en luminosité, si ces derniers sont associés à des tissus aux tons chauds.
Schlafzimmer mit Holzmöbeln oder schokoladenbraunen Möbeln wirk heller, wenn sie mit Textilien in warmen Farben dekoriert sind.

284 Red goes very well with stone or polished gray concrete.
Le rouge se marie très bien à la pierre ou au ciment ciré gris.
Rot passt gut zu Naturstein und zu grauem Zementglattstrich.

© Gregory Goode

5 Rooms with mauve walls and white furniture convey serenity.
Les pièces où les murs sont mauves et les meubles blancs dégagent une impression de sérénité.
Räume mit malvenfarbigen Wänden und weißen Möbeln strahlen Gelassenheit aus.

6 Orange is a good counterpoint to steel finishings.
La couleur orange offre un contraste intéressant aux revêtements en acier.
Orange ist ein guter Gegensatz zu Stahlverkleidungen.

7 A child's bedroom is brighter and cozier with warm colors thinned down to pastel shades.
Parée de couleurs chaleureuses nuancées de tons pastel, la chambre d'enfants gagne en luminosité et chaleur.
Ein Kinderzimmer wirkt heller und wärmer in warmen Farben, die mit Pastelltönen abgeschwächt sind.

8 There is less risk of a space looking small when glossy materials are used.
Avec des matériaux brillants, les risques de rapetisser les pièces sont moindres.
Mit glänzenden Materialien ist das Risiko, dass der Raum kleiner wirkt, geringer.

289 Lamps that emit warm colors are only suitable for partial or decorative lighting.
Les lampes qui diffusent des couleurs chaudes sont uniquement recommandées pour l'éclairage décoratif ou partiel.
Lampen, die Licht in warmen Farben ausstrahlen, sind eine gute Lösung für die Dekoration oder Teilbeleuchtung bestimmter Zonen.

290 Yellow or soft orange ceilings make spaces covered in wood appear larger.
Les plafonds de couleur jaune ou orange suave agrandissent visuellement les espaces lambrissés.
Gelbe oder hellorange Decken lassen mit Holz verkleidete Räume größer wirken.

© Luuk Kramer

© Luuk Kramer

291 Pale shades of cool colors convey freshness and expansiveness, so th
help make rooms look bigger.
Les couleurs froides dans des nuances claires déclinent fraîcheur et
sensation d'espace, contribuant ainsi à agrandir les pièces.
Kalte helle Farben wirken frisch und erweiternd, so dass die Räume
optisch an Größe gewinnen.

292 The combination of acid green on furniture and steel on walls is vibran
and luminous; it is guaranteed to enliven small kitchens.
Le vert acidulé du mobilier et l'acier des murs forment une associatio
vibrante et lumineuse qui éveille les petites cuisines.
Gelbgrün an den Möbeln und Stahl an den Wänden ist eine kraftvolle
und leuchtende Kombination, die kleine Küchen belebt.

293 Blue and white striped wallpaper with a nautical feel adds style to roor
with low ceilings.
Les papiers muraux à rayures blanches et bleues, inspirés du style
marin, permettent de styliser les pièces basses de plafond.
Tapeten mit weißen und blauen Streifen im Marinestil lassen Räume m
niedrigen Decken stilvoll wirken.

294 Blue conveys serenity. A frieze in this color is ideal for a child's bedro
when applied to a white wall with paint or paper.
Le bleu confère sérénité. La création d'une frise dans cette couleur,
peinte ou en papier sur un mur blanc est parfaite pour une chambre
d'enfants.

© Luuk Kramer

Die Farbe Blau strahlt Gelassenheit aus. Ein blauer Zierstreifen auf einer weißen Wand, entweder gemalt oder tapeziert, ist ein sehr schönes Dekorationselement für Kinderzimmer.

Small bathrooms seem bigger if the floor is colored turquoise green and the walls are coated with polished cement.
Les petites salles de bains s'amplifient si le sol et les murs de ciment ciré et poli sont teints en vert turquoise.
Kleine Bäder wirken größer, wenn man einen türkisen Boden verlegt und die Wände mit Zementglattstrich verkleidet.

Wallpaper with pale green and blue designs creates settings with a retro look.
Le papier peint à graphiques vert clair et bleu crée des ambiances style rétro.
Tapeten mit grafischen Mustern in Hellgrün und Blau lassen eine Wohnumgebung im Retrostil entstehen.

Modern kitchens look good with mosaic floors and walls in various shades of blue and green.
Les cuisines modernes tolèrent les sols et murs de mosaïques dans différents tons de bleu et vert.
In modernen Küchen kann man Böden und Wände mit Mosaiken in verschiedenen Blau- und Grüntönen schmücken.

298 A sitting room seems more spacious if one wall is papered with plant motifs and the others are painted white.
Le salon gagne de l'espace avec un mur revêtu en papier peint aux motifs végétaux, et le reste peint en blanc.
Das Wohnzimmer wirkt größer, wenn man eine Wand mit Pflanzenmotiven tapeziert und die übrigen weiß streicht.

299 A dark blue carpet does not affect the visual perception of a room's dimensions if it is combined with totally white walls.
Une moquette bleu foncé n'affecte pas les dimensions visuelles d'une pièce si les murs sont totalement blancs.
Dunkelblauer Teppichboden macht die Räume optisch nicht kleiner, wenn man dazu völlig weiße Wände wählt.

300 Cool colors provide a counterpoint for rooms exposed to direct sunlight.
Les couleurs froides offrent un contraste dans les pièces où la lumière solaire entre directement.
Kalte Farben eignen sich gut für Räume, in die direktes Sonnenlicht fällt.

© Hanse Haus

© Bjorg Arnasdot

301   Neutral colors – running across the range of browns, grays, whites and beige – induce serenity.
Les couleurs neutres, composées d'une gamme de marron, gris, blanc et beige, diffusent une ambiance de sérénité.
Neutrale Farben, zu denen die verschiedenen Braun-, Grau-, Weiß- und Beigetöne gehören, strahlen Gelassenheit aus.

302   Gray borders on the cooler colors. To counteract this effect, it must be combined with warm colors like red, pink, yellow and orange.
Le gris tend vers les tons froids. Pour contrecarrer cet effet, lui associe des tons chauds comme le rouge, le rose, le jaune et l'orange.
Grau ist eher ein kalter Farbton. Deshalb sollte es mit warmen Farben wie Rot, Rosa, Gelb oder Orange kombiniert werden.

303   Brown is closer to the warm colors and establishes a modern, elegant contrast with pale blue.
Le marron se rapproche des couleurs chaudes et s'inscrit en contraste élégant et moderne avec le bleu clair.
Braun ist eher eine warme Farbe und stellt einen eleganten und modernen Kontrast zu Hellblau dar.

304   Neutral-colored furniture is ideal for all small spaces.
Les meubles de couleur neutre sont la base de tous les espaces de petites dimensions.
Möbel in neutralen Farben eignen sich ausgezeichnet für kleine Räume

© Hisao Suzuki

When a space is dominated by neutral colors, the remaining colors are activated.

Une prépondérance des tons neutres dans une pièce, met en valeur les autres couleurs.

Wenn neutrale Farben in der Dekoration vorherrschen, haben die übrigen Farben mehr Kraft.

Neutral colors are appropriate for disguising beams, pillars and other structural elements.

Ce sont les couleurs qu'il convient d'utiliser pour masquer poutres, piliers et autres éléments structuraux de la maison.

Mit neutralen Farben kann man Balken, Säulen und andere strukturelle Elemente des Hauses besser in der Umgebung verschwinden lassen.

A totally white home looks big but loses personality, so it is advisable to add splashes of color in the furniture, fabrics and lighting.

Une maison entièrement blanche gagne en espace mais perd en caractère. Recourir alors à la couleur du mobilier, des tissus et de l'éclairage.

Eine völlig weiße Wohnung wirkt geräumig, hat aber keinen Eigencharakter. In diesem Fall kann man mit der Farbe der Möbel, der Textilien und der Beleuchtung, die Dekoration persönlicher gestalten.

Wallpaper with reliefs and neutral colors sets up interesting interplays of textures.

Les papiers muraux aux couleurs neutres et en relief provoquent d'intéressants jeux de textures.

Tapeten in neutralen Farben mit Reliefen lassen interessante Wirkungen der Texturen entstehen.

309 White lacquer can add luminosity when applied to wooden bookshelves and tables in a setting dominated by dark concrete.

Les étagères et tables en bois laqué, de couleur blanche, confèrent luminosité aux pièces dominées par le ciment foncé.

Weiß lackierte Regale und Holztische lassen Wohnungen, in denen dunkler Zement dominiert, heller wirken.

310 A selection of neutral colors establishes contrasts without reducing the sense of spaciousness.

Les différents tons neutres créent des contrastes sans pour autant diminuer la sensation d'espace.

Die verschiedenen neutralen Farben stellen Kontraste her, lassen den Raum aber nie kleiner wirken.

© Reto Guntli, Agi Simoes / Zapaimag

© Luis He

© Luuk Kramer

311 The combination of black and white is a classic with elegance. The respective proportions of the two colors depend on the size of the room.
Le binôme noir et blanc est un modèle d'élégance. La prépondérance d'une couleur ou d'une autre dépend de la taille des pièces.
Die Kombination von Schwarz und Weiß ist ein Klassiker der eleganter Dekoration. Ob die eine oder die andere der beiden Farben vorherrschen sollte, hängt von der Raumgröße ab.

312 A home acquires a loft feel when decorated with wooden floors, white walls and black furniture with metal finishing.
Les maisons prennent des allures de loft avec des parquets, des murs blancs et un mobilier noir agrémenté de métal.
Wohnungen wirken wie eine Fabriketage, wenn der Boden aus Holz ist die Wände weiß und die Möbel schwarz mit Elementen aus Metall.

313 The conjunction of complementary colors does not diminish the sense of spaciousness and emphasizes a home's fresh, youthful character.
Le mélange de couleurs complémentaires n'affecte pas l'espace et renforce le côté jeune et frais d'une habitation.
Die Zusammenstellung von Komplementärfarben wirkt sich nicht negativ auf die Raumempfindung aus und lässt jede Wohnung jung und frisch aussehen.

314 Built-in kitchens with an orange wall and blue closets provide harmonious results in a living room covered with gray stone.

Les cuisines américaines, au mur de couleur orange et aux armoires bleues, se marient à merveille avec un salon habillé de pierre grise.

Offene Küchen mit einer orangefarbenen Wand und gelben Schränken fügen sich harmonisch ins Gesamtbild, wenn das Wohnzimmer mit grauem Naturstein verkleidet ist.

5 To make elongated rooms look wider, it is advisable to paint the biggest walls red and the smaller ones white.

Pour élargir visuellement les pièces en longueur, peindre de rouge les murs plus grands et de blanc les plus petits.

Um längliche Räume optisch größer wirken zu lassen, sollte man die größeren Wände rot und die kleineren weiß streichen.

6 Vinyl flooring in complementary colors like green and pink is ideal for long, dark corridors.

Les revêtements en vinyle pour un appartement aux couleurs complémentaires comme le vert et le rose sont parfaits pour les longs couloirs sombres.

Für lange und dunkle Flure eignen sich ausgezeichnet Vinylfußböden in Komplementärfarben wie Grün und Rosa.

7 If a bedroom is painted green to make it look bigger, its coldness can be offset by a mauve bedcover and red lampshades.

Si la chambre à coucher est peinte en vert pour gagner de l'espace, contrebalancer la froideur de cette couleur par des édredons mauves et des lampes à abat-jour rouge.

Wenn das Schlafzimmer grün gestrichen ist, damit es größer wirkt, kann man die Kälte dieser Farbe mit blasslila Bettüberwürfen und Lampen mit roten Schirmen ausgleichen.

318 Black woolen rugs define different settings in a single-space home with white walls and ceilings.

Les tapis de laine teints en noir définissent les pièces dans les maisons à espace unique doté de murs et plafonds blancs.

Schwarz gefärbte Wollteppiche definieren Bereiche in einer Wohnung mit nur einem einzigen Raum, die weiße Wände und Decken haben.

319 Wallpaper with designs featuring black-and-white optical effects makes the surface area of walls seem bigger.

Le papier peint avec des dessins à effet optique noir et blanc agrandit la surface des murs.

Tapeten mit schwarzweißen Motiven und optischem Effekt lassen die Wände größer wirken.

320 Small sitting rooms can support neo-baroque decoration if there is a predominance of yellow on the walls and purple on the decorative details.

Les petits salons supportent la décoration néo-baroque à condition que le jaune domine sur les murs et le pourpre sur les détails décoratifs.

Kleine Wohnzimmer dürfen im neobarocken Stil dekoriert werden, wenn Gelb an den Wänden und Purpurrot in den Dekorationselementen dominiert.

© Luuk Kramer

© Jordi Miralles

© Hisao Suzuki

Nuria Fuent

321 The conjunction of colors that are close to each other on the color wheel gives a space harmony.

La présence de couleurs proches dans une gamme chromatique crée des univers harmonieux.

Durch die Verwendung von Farben, die im Farbkreis nicht weit voneinander entfernt sind, entstehen harmonische Wohnumgebungen.

322 A sitting room in a single-space home can be defined by a range of red oranges and yellows on the couch, carpet and cushions.

Pour définir un salon dans une maison à espace unique, recourir à la gamme de rouge, orange et jaune pour le divan, le tapis et les coussin

Um ein Wohnzimmer in einer Wohnung mit nur einem Raum zu definieren, kann man die Rot-, Orange- und Gelbtöne für das Sofa, den Teppich und die Kissen benutzen.

323 A bedroom with gray stone on its walls and floor can become cozier with the addition of a violet-colored bedcover, a blue blanket and a green carpe

La chambre à coucher, dotée de murs et sol de pierre grise, devient plus accueillante avec un édredon violet, une couverture bleue et un tapis ve

Ein Schlafzimmer mit Wänden und Boden aus grauem Stein wirkt mit einer Steppdecke in Violett, einer blauen Decke und einem grünen Teppich gemütlich.

324 A house acquires a greater sense of depth if the walls near its entrance are painted in bright colors like red and blue, before moving on to pale colors like yellow and lilac at the other end of the home.

© Jordi Miralles

© Jordi Miralles

La maison gagne en profondeur si les murs de l'entrée sont peints en couleurs plus intenses (comme le rouge ou le bleu), pour finir avec un ton plus clair (jaune ou violet) à l'autre bout de la demeure.
Die Wohnung wirkt tiefer, wenn die Wände am Eingang in starken Farben (wie Rot oder Blau) gestrichen sind, und das andere Ende der Wohnung in helleren Farben (wie Gelb oder Lila).

25 One way of separating a living area from a dining room is by painting the walls of each space with similar colors on the color wheel.
Une manière de séparer le salon de la salle à manger est de peindre les murs de chaque zone dans un camaïeu de couleurs proches.
Eine Möglichkeit, das Wohnzimmer vom Speisezimmer abzutrennen, ist es, die Wände in jedem Bereich in Farben zu streichen, die sich im Farbkreis nahe liegen.

26 To make long corridors look shorter, choose a bright color for the far end and a pastel color for the walls (e.g. red and pink).
Pour couper les couloirs très longs, choisir pour le fond une couleur intense et pour les murs un ton pastel : par exemple, rouge et rose.
Um lange Flure kürzer wirken zu lassen, sollte der Hintergrund in einer intensiven Farbe und die Wände in Pastellfarben gestrichen werden, zum Beispiel Rot und Rosa.

27 In contrast, to make a corridor look bigger, the walls and far end should be painted in a pale color, such as acid green, and the ceiling in a dark color, such as blue.

Au contraire, pour élargir le couloir, peindre le fond d'un ton clair, en vert acidulé, par exemple, et les plafonds et murs plus foncés, en bleu.
Wenn man einen Flur weiter wirken lassen will, sollte man die Wand im Hintergrund in einer hellen Farbe wie Gelbgrün streichen, und die Decke und Wände in einer dunklen, zum Beispiel Blau.

328 To create a restful atmosphere in a bedroom, wallpaper can be combined with paint in adjoining colors on the color wheel.
Pour favoriser le repos, le revêtement en papier peint de la chambre à coucher doit se marier avec des murs aux couleurs de la même gamme.
Damit das Schlafzimmer ruhiger wirkt, sollte man die Schlafzimmertapeten in Farben wählen, die sich auf dem Farbkreis nahe sind.

329 Redbrick rooms look bigger with wooden floors that stretch across the range of ochers.
Les espaces en brique rouge deviennent plus grands avec des parquets dans différentes nuances d'ocre.
Wohnungen mit rotem Ziegelstein wirken mit Holzböden in Ockerfarben größer.

330 Poufs and cushions are ideal for bringing the color wheel full circle in a sitting room.
Les poufs et les coussins sont idéals pour compléter la gamme chromatique des salons.
Sitzkissen und Kissen eignen sich ausgezeichnet, um den Farbkreis in Wohnzimmern zu vervollständigen.

Furniture
Équipement
Ausstattung

Although it may seem that large pieces of furniture make a space look smaller, in fact a limited number of such items can make rooms look more open. It is all a question of scale, which can be resolved by planning and ingenuity, based on the array of possibilities currently on the market.

D'habitude on pense que les meubles de grandes tailles rapetissent les pièces, pourtant quelques grands meubles agrandiront l'espace. Il s'agit en fait d'une question de dosage dans l'équipement de la maison, facile à résoudre par le biais d'un aménagement astucieux utilisant les diverses possibilités offertes par les fabricants.

Auch wenn man glauben könnte, dass größere Möbel einen Raum kleiner wirken lassen, ist es doch so, dass wenige große Möbelstücke ihn offener machen. Es geht also darum, das richtige Verhältnis zu finden, und unter dem großen Angebot der verschiedenen Hersteller gekonnt das Richtige zu wählen.

© David Frutos, Adhoc MSL

© Margherita Spilutt

© Guy Wenborne

331 Entrance halls are usually small spaces and are thus unsuitable for lar
pieces of furniture.
Les vestibules sont en général des petits espaces, où les meubles
encombrants sont à bannir.
Flure sind meist sehr klein, deshalb sollte man dort keine großen Möb
aufstellen.

332 A large mirror with a thick wooden frame standing on the floor in a
spotlight is sufficient to make an entrance look bigger.
Un grand miroir avec un cadre de bois large, posé sur le sol et illuminé
par une source lumineuse, suffit pour agrandir l'entrée.
Ein großer Spiegel mit einem breiten Holzrahmen, der sich auf den
Boden stützt, und einem Strahler, der diesen beleuchtet, reicht aus, ur
den Eingangsbereich geräumig wirken zu lassen.

333 Coat stands take up room, while hooks on the wall keep the floor free
and bring a greater sense of spaciousness.
Les portemanteaux sur pied prennent de la place. Par contre, ceux qui
sont accrochés au mur, dégagent le sol, et accentuent ainsi la sensatic
d'espace.
Kleiderständer nehmen Platz weg. Wandgarderoben lassen den Boden
frei, wodurch der Raum optisch größer wirkt.

334 Units with long, narrow drawers add a touch of style to a hallway and
provide a base for a vase in a color that contrasts with the wall.

© Margherita Spiluttini

Les commodes à tiroirs étroits et allongés stylisent les vestibules et permettent de poser un vase de couleur offrant un contraste avec le mur.
Schränke mit schmalen, länglichen Schubladen machen den Eingangsbereich stilvoller und man kann farbige Krüge darauf stellen, die einen Kontrast zur Wand bilden.

5 Both the hall and the corridors should have several sources of light.
Le vestibule et les couloirs doivent être dotés de diverses sources de lumière.
Sowohl im Eingangsbereich als auch in den Fluren sollte es verschiedene Lichtquellen geben.

6 A hall looks bigger by adding of a large standard lamp to a furniture unit.
Pour que le vestibule paraisse plus spacieux, installer une lampe de grande taille au-dessus de la console.
Damit der Eingangsbereich geräumiger wirkt, stellen Sie eine einzige große Stehlampe auf die Konsole.

7 The visual perception of a long corridor can be shortened by placing an arrangement of pictures of different sizes (but all framed in the same color).
Les compositions de divers tableaux de tailles différentes mais encadrés dans une même couleur coupent les longs couloirs.

Lange Flure wirken kürzer, wenn man Bilder in verschiedenen Größen, aber mit dem selben Rahmen aufhängt.

338 Transparent metacrylate units are ideally suited to the far end of a short corridor.
Les consoles en méthacrylate transparent sont idéales pour meubler le fond des couloirs trop courts.
Konsolen aus transparentem Metacrylat eignen sich ideal für den hinteren Teil eines kurzen Flurs.

339 Coat stands fitted with a shelf provide a space for leaving letters and keys in the hall.
Les portemanteaux à étagères permettent de déposer le courrier et les clés dans le vestibule.
Garderoben mit Regalen schaffen Platz, um die Post und die Schlüssel abzulegen.

340 If a corridor has one or several windows, the lower part of the opening can be used as a platform for pots with small-leaved plants.
Si le couloir possède une ou diverses fenêtres, on peut profiter du rebord inférieur de l'ouverture pour poser des pots de fleurs ou des plantes à petites feuilles.
Wenn es in dem Flur ein oder mehrere Fenster gibt, kann am unteren Teil des Fensters ein Fensterbrett für Blumentöpfe mit immergrünen Pflanzen montiert werden.

© Stefan Me

© Shania Shegedyn

341 A couch can be the focal point of a small sitting room and does not necessarily have to be small itself.

Le divan placé dans un petit espace ne doit pas être nécessairement petit si c'est le meuble principal du salon.

Ein Sofa in einem kleinen Raum muss nicht unbedingt klein sein, wen es das dominierende Möbelstück im Wohnzimmer ist.

342 Straight-line couches take up less space because they are low and compact.

Bas et compacts, les divans aux lignes droites prennent moins de plac

Sofas in geraden Linien nehmen weniger Platz weg, weil sie niedriger und kompakter sind.

343 When a sitting room is too small to take more than one couch, poufs can serve as a practical complement.

Si les dimensions du salon ne tolèrent qu'un divan, les poufs devienne alors des éléments d'appoint pratiques.

Wenn in ein kleines Wohnzimmer nicht mehr als ein Sofa passt, eigne sich Puffs als praktische Ergänzung.

344 Modular couches that include a chaise longue, complemented by a small table in the place of an armrest, can adapt their shape to the space available.

Les divans modulaires qui permettent d'intégrer un élément *chaise longue*, en plus d'une petite table en guise d'accoudoir, adaptent leur forme à l'espace.

© Murray Fredericks

Modulare Sofas, in die man eine Chaiselongue integrieren kann, und anstatt der Armlehnen einen kleinen Tisch, lassen sich an jegliche Raumform anpassen.

Metal and wood armrests add a touch of style to couches.
Les accoudoirs métalliques ou en bois stylisent les divans.
Armlehnen aus Metall oder Holz lassen die Sofas edler wirken.

The latest trends in decoration set great resort to contrasts and have revived the Louis-XV armchair, upholstered and painted in a single color for minimalist settings.
Dans le domaine de la décoration, les tendances en vogue ont recours aux contrastes et récupèrent le fauteuil Louis XV en le tapissant et le peignant d'une même couleur pour meubler les univers minimalistes.
Der neuste Trend in der Dekoration geht in Richtung Kontraste. Gepolsterte und in der gleichen Farbe gestrichene Sessel im Stil Ludwig XV. stehen in minimalistischen Wohnungen.

7   Small armchairs complemented by a standard lamp create a reading area in a bedroom.
Dans la chambre à coucher, les petits fauteuils dotés d'une lampe créent un mini espace de lecture.
Im Schlafzimmer entsteht durch kleine Sessel mit einer Stehlampe ein kleiner Lesebereich.

348   It is advisable to acquire a fold-out couch when a home has no guest bedroom.
Si la maison ne dispose pas de chambre d'amis, opter pour un divan lit.
Wenn es in der Wohnung kein Gästezimmer gibt, sollte man ein Bettsofa haben.

349   Footrest modules with storage space underneath are ideal for storing magazines or toys.
Les modules de repose-pieds avec un espace de rangement sous le siège sont idéals pour ranger revues ou jouets.
Fußstützenmodule mit Lagerraum unter dem Sitz eignen sich ideal zum Aufbewahren von Zeitschriften und Spielzeug.

350   Vertical stripes stylize a couch, whereas small squares make it look bigger.
Les rayures verticales stylisent un divan, alors que les petits carrés l'agrandissent visuellement.
Vertikale Streifen lassen das Sofa edel wirken, und kleine Quadrate machen es optisch größer.

© Jordi Miral

© Shania Shegedyn

351 Trunks or old leather suitcases can double as coffee tables and storag units.

Les coffres ou les anciennes valises en cuir peuvent servir de tables basses et de meubles de rangement.

Truhen und alte Koffer dienen gleichzeitig als Couchtisch und als Lagerraum.

352 Extremely small rooms call for very low coffee tables.

Les très petites pièces requièrent des tables très basses.

In kleinen Zimmern müssen die Couchtische sehr niedrig sein.

353 Coffee tables with a shelf underneath can be used to hold magazines or DVDs. Others are fitted with large drawers that are perfect for stori blankets and pillows.

Les tables qui ont un rayonnage en dessous permettent de ranger les revues ou les DVD. Celles qui ont des tiroirs plus spacieux sont idéale pour ranger couvertures et coussins.

Tische mit einem Regal unter der Tischfläche eignen sich zum Aufbewahren von Zeitschriften und DVDs. Und Tische mit größeren Schubladen sind ideal für Decken und Kissen.

354 Table nests, made up of three successively smaller tables, do not take up any space when they are fitted together but can adapt to every nee

Les tables gigognes, composées de trois pièces de plus en plus petite une fois emboîtées, ne prennent pas de place et s'adaptent en fonctio des besoins spontanés.

© Matteo Piazza

Stapelbare Beistelltische in verschiedenen, ineinander passenden Größen nehmen wenig Platz weg und eignen sich für verschiedene Zwecke.

5   Metacrylate coffee tables are now very fashionable; their transparency means that they do not constitute a visual obstacle.
Les tables basses en méthacrylate sont le dernier cri : transparentes, elles libèrent l'espace sans le gêner.
Tische aus Metacrylat sind zur Zeit sehr modern, weil sie transparent sind und kein visuelles Hindernis darstellen.

6   Round coffee tables are easier to fit into small spaces than rectangular ones.
Les tables basses rondes sont plus faciles à intégrer dans les petits univers que les rectangulaires.
Runde Tische passen besser in kleine Räume als quadratische.

7   Coffee tables with square stools that can be tucked underneath serve as an informal eating area.
Les tables basses avec des tabourets carrés qui s'encastrent dessous, servent de salle à manger informelles.
Couchtische mit quadratischen Ständern, die man darunter einhaken kann, können auch als unkonventioneller Essplatz dienen.

358   A sense of spaciousness can be achieved by choosing a coffee table in a lighter color than the couch.
Pour accentuer la sensation d'espace, choisir la couleur de la table basse plus claire que celle du divan.
Damit der Raum größer wirkt, sollte die Farbe des Sofatisches heller als die des Sofas sein.

359   In settings with a matt finish (such as concrete), tables made of glass and brushed steel help to reflect light.
Dans les espaces habillés de revêtements patinés, comme le béton, les tables conjuguant acier brossé et verre reflètent la lumière.
In Wohnungen mit matten Verkleidungen, wie Beton, reflektieren Tische aus gebürstetem Stahl und Glas das Licht.

360   Transparent coffee tables with a light inside add a designer touch to sitting rooms whose dimensions do not permit the presence of a lot of furniture.
Dans les salons dont les dimensions ne tolèrent que peu de meubles, les tables transparentes munies d'une lumière interne apportent une touche de design.
In Wohnzimmern, in die nur wenig Möbel passen, bilden transparente Tische mit Innenbeleuchtung ein modernes und auffallendes Dekorationselement.

© Pep Esco

© Angelo Kaunat

© Joan Roig

© Yael Pincus

© Eric Koya

© Ake Eson Lindmann

361 Tables with a single central support leave more space for chairs and more unobtrusive.

Les tables avec un seul pied central, dégagent l'espace pour les sièges et paraissent plus transparentes.

Tische mit einem einzigen, zentralen Tischbein lassen mehr Platz für Stühle und wirken leichter.

362 Folding tables and chairs can be stored in a corner when not in use.

Les tables et sièges pliables peuvent être rangés dans un coin si on ne les utilise pas.

Klapptische und Klappstühle können in einer Ecke abgestellt werden, wenn man sie nicht benötigt.

363 Tables with extending leaves and stackable chairs save space and can adapt to varying numbers of guests.

Les tables à rallonge et les sièges empilables offrent un gain d'espace et s'adaptent à un nombre variable de convives.

Ausziehbare Tische und Stapelstühle helfen Platz zu sparen und passen sich an die Zahl der Tischgäste an.

364 The transparent polycarbonate furniture pioneered by Philippe Starck helps bring a sense of spaciousness to dark dining rooms.

Le mobilier en polycarbonate transparent, mis à la mode par Philippe Starck, accentue la sensation d'espace dans les salles à manger sombres.

© Jürg Zimmermann

Philippe Starck war Trendsetter mit seinen Möbeln aus transparentem Polykarbonat, die dunkle Esszimmer heller machen.

A round table not only occupies less space but also defines a dining area more clearly when the latter is integrated into a sitting room.
Quand la salle à manger est intégrée au salon, les tables rondes occupent moins d'espace et en plus délimitent mieux les zones de vie.
Wenn das Esszimmer zum Wohnzimmer gehört, sollten die Tische rund sein. Sie nehmen nicht nur weniger Platz weg, sondern sie grenzen auch besser den Essbereich ab.

If a room is very small, it is advisable to use stools instead of chairs.
Si la pièce est très petite, utiliser des tabourets en guise de sièges.
Wenn der Raum sehr klein ist, sollte man Hocker statt Stühle aufstellen.

Gate-leg tables do not take up space when folded against a wall.
Une fois pliées contre le mur, les tables convertibles ne prennent pas de place.
Klapptische nehmen keinen Platz weg, wenn sie gegen die Wand geklappt werden.

High-back chairs constitute a visual obstacle and make rooms look smaller.
Les sièges au dossier très haut entravent la vue et rapetissent les pièces.

Stühle mit sehr hohen Rückenlehnen sind ein visuelles Hindernis und lassen den Raum kleiner wirken.

369 Metal legs make dining room tables and chairs less eye-catching.
Les pieds métalliques des tables et sièges de salle à manger allègent visuellement le mobilier.
Metallfüße an Tischen und Stühlen im Esszimmer lassen die Möbel leichter wirken.

370 It is a good idea to choose chairs with backs that fit snugly against the sides of the table, in order to save space when they are tucked underneath.
Opter pour des sièges à dossiers encastrables dans les angles de la table pour gagner de l'espace quand on les range.
Man sollte die Stühle so wählen, dass sich ihre Stuhllehnen an die Ecken des Tisches anpassen, dann kann man sie besser an den Tisch schieben.

© Jürg Zimmermann

371 Open bookcases that allow light to pass through are ideal for dividing spaces.

Les bibliothèques ouvertes, qui laissent circuler la lumière, sont parfaites pour diviser les espaces de vie.

Offene Regale, die Licht durchlassen, eignen sich ausgezeichnet als Raumteiler.

372 Shelves fixed to a wall can be used to take advantage of the space between the top of a door and the ceiling.

Les rayonnages qui se fixent au mur permettent d'utiliser l'espace qui reste entre le plafond et le haut des portes.

Mit Regalbrettern an der Wand nutzt man den Platz zwischen der Decke und dem oberen Teil der Türen besser aus.

373 Steel frames with ash-wood shelves have a light structure that appear not to take up much room.

Les étagères d'acier avec rayonnages en bois de hêtre sont des structures légères qui n'encombrent pas l'espace.

Regale mit Stahlgerüst und Buchenholzablagen wirken so leicht, dass sie keinen Raum einzunehmen scheinen.

374 Adjustable shelves open up spaces in a bookcase devoted to several uses and can thus make room for a television, books or ornaments.

Les rayonnages réglables créent des espaces dans l'étagère à usages divers : la télévision, les livres et les accessoires décoratifs.

Einstellbare Regalbretter schaffen Platz in Regalen, die verschiedenen

© Margherita Spilutti

Zwecken dienen, wie zum Beispiel der Aufnahme des Fernsehers, der Bücher und verschiedener Dekorationsobjekte.

All narrow spaces can be exploited by installing vertical bookcases, but their color must be similar or identical to that of the wall.
Profiter de tous les espaces étroits pour disposer des étagères verticales, en s'assurant que leur couleur est identique à celle du mur.
Enge Flächen kann man für vertikale Regale nutzen. Es ist jedoch wichtig, dass sie die gleiche oder eine ähnliche Farbe wie die Wand haben.

Covered shelf units are ideal for storing toys on the walls of a child's bedroom, as uncluttered floors give a greater sense of spaciousness.
Les étagères suspendues à rabats sont parfaites pour ranger les jouets dans la chambre à coucher des enfants : les sols ainsi libérés, accentuent la sensation d'espace.
Hängeregale mit Abdeckungen eignen sich ausgezeichnet, um Spielsachen im Kinderzimmer aufzubewahren. So bleibt der Boden frei und im Zimmer ist mehr Platz.

One or two shelves with a metal grille can serve to store towels in a bathroom.
Une ou deux étagères en maille métallique dans la salle de bains permettent de ranger les serviettes.
Ein oder zwei Regale mit Metallgittern im Bad dienen zum Aufbewahren der Handtücher.

378   Very small kitchens that have no space for closets (apart from underneath the worktop) can be equipped with wide shelves fitted against the walls.
Les cuisines très petites qui n'ont de place que pour accueillir des placards sous le plan de travail, peuvent se rabattre sur des larges étagères adossées au mur.
In sehr kleinen Küchen, in denen es nur Platz für Regale unter den Arbeitsflächen gibt, kann man breite Regale an die Wand lehnen.

379   Narrow bookcases set on their side with rollers can be used as a storage unit that can be moved when a particular object is required.
Les étagères étroites latérales et à roulettes fonctionnent comme des grands tiroirs qui se déploient uniquement pour prendre un objet.
Enge, seitlich aufgestellte Regale mit Rädern dienen als große Kisten, die man nur herauszieht, wenn man etwas herausnehmen will.

380   Bookshelves spread across an entire wall have the advantage of concentrating a sitting room's storage requirements in a single module.
Les étagères qui occupent le mur entier offrent l'avantage de réunir en un seul module tous les besoins de rangement du salon.
Regale, die eine ganze Wand einnehmen, haben den Vorteil, dass man in einem einzigen Modul den gesamten Lagerraum für die Ausstattung des Wohnzimmers findet.

© Ake Eson Lindmann

© Nuria Fuen

© Ángel Baltanás

© Trevor Main

381 Closets with sliding doors can be placed very close to a bed, leaving just enough room to pass by.
Les armoires à portes coulissantes peuvent être placées très près du lit laissant seulement un passage pour circuler.
Schränke mit Schiebetüren kann man ganz nah am Bett aufstellen und nur einen schmalen Durchgang freilassen.

382 Wall closets fixed above the headboard in a narrow bedroom act as a complement to the focal point of the bed.
Dans les chambres étroites, les armoires murales qui s'accrochent au-dessus de la tête de lit complètent le meuble principal.
In engen Zimmern dient ein hängender Wandschrank über dem Kopfteil des Bettes als Ergänzung zu dem Hauptmöbel.

383 Mirrored doors make a room look bigger.
Les portes miroirs agrandissent la chambre.
Türen mit Spiegeln lassen den Raum größer wirken.

384 All the dead spaces in a home – such as the areas under a staircase or between the beams and the wall – can be used to install closets.
Tous les angles morts de la maison, comme l'espace sous l'escalier ou celui qui reste entre les poutres et le mur, peuvent être utilisés pour installer des placards.
Alle toten Winkel eines Hauses wie der Platz unter der Treppe oder zwischen den Balken und der Wand können für Schränke genutzt werden.

© Shania Shegedyn

5 Built-in closets have the great advantage of not stealing any space from other furniture and thus making a room look bigger.
Les armoires encastrées offrent l'immense avantage de libérer l'espace pour les autres meubles et agrandissent les pièces.
Einbauschränke bieten den großen Vorteil, dass sie den anderen Möbeln keinen Platz wegnehmen und lassen die Räume optisch größer wirken.

6 It is advisable for closets in a corridor to be made of a pale wood that provides luminosity.
Installer dans les couloirs des armoires réalisées dans un bois clair pour apporter de la luminosité.
Schränke in Fluren sollten aus hellem Holz sein, so wirkt der Raum heller.

7 Doors do not obstruct closets if they share the same wall, as the latter can continue above the door frame.
Les portes n'entravent pas les placards lorsqu'ils partagent le même mur, car le meuble peut se prolonger au-dessus de l'encadrement de la porte.
Türen sind keine Hindernisse für Schränke, wenn sie sich an der gleichen Wand befinden, da letztere über dem Türrahmen fortgesetzt werden können.

8 In single-space homes, closets can function as a dividing panel in a bedroom; in this case, it is important for the rear of the closet to be covered in keeping with its surroundings.

Dans les maisons à espace unique, les armoires peuvent servir de cloison pour séparer la chambre à coucher. Le revêtement du dos de l'armoire doit alors être en harmonie avec la partie attenante.
In Wohnungen mit nur einem einzigen Raum können Schränke als Raumteiler zum Schlafzimmer hin dienen. In diesem Fall wurde die Rückseite des Schrankes wie der angrenzende Schlafbereich dekoriert.

389 To make the most of a child's bedroom, a closet can be set underneath a bed, which in turn can be fitted with a small ladder.
Pour optimiser la chambre à coucher des enfants, installer un placard sous le lit auquel on accède par une petite échelle.
Um ein Kinderzimmer so gut wie möglich auszunutzen, kann man einen Schrank unter dem Bett anstellen. Ins Bett führt eine Leiter.

390 Closets with glass doors that expose the back wall make a kitchen look bigger.
Les armoires de cuisine aux portes en verre laissant voir le mur agrandissent la pièce.
Küchenschränke mit Glastüren, durch die man die Wand sieht, lassen die Küche größer wirken.

© Ángel Baltaná

© Pep Escoda

391 Beds with drawers underneath obviate the need for chests of drawers other complementary furniture.

Les lits munis de tiroirs dans la partie inférieure permettent de se passer de commodes ou de meubles d'appoint.

Betten mit Schubladen machen es möglich, auf Kommoden und andere zusätzliche Möbelstücke zu verzichten.

392 If a mattress is placed on top of a platform, not only does it leave more free space but it also allows the wooden structure to be used for storage.

Installer le matelas au-dessus d'une estrade, dégage à la fois l'espace tout en permettant de profiter de la structure en bois pour le rangement.

Wenn man die Matratze auf ein Podium legt, hat man nicht nur mehr freien Platz, sondern man kann die Holzstruktur auch als Lagerraum nutzen.

393 High beds that are reached via a ladder make it possible to put a couch or desk underneath.

Les lits élevés, munis d'une échelle pour y accéder, permettent d'accueillir dessous un divan ou un bureau.

Hohe Betten, in die man über eine Leiter gelangt, machen es möglich, darunter ein Sofa oder einen Schreibtisch aufzustellen.

394 Extendable beds of variable lengths help to free up a play area in a child's bedroom.

© Paul Ott

© Nuria Fuentes

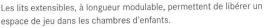

Les lits extensibles, à longueur modulable, permettent de libérer un espace de jeu dans les chambres d'enfants.
Ausziehbare Betten gibt es in verschiedenen Längen. Mit diesen Betten gewinnt man in Kinderzimmern Platz zum Spielen.

395 If the wall above a bed is clad with upholstered leather, there is no need for any cumbersome headboard.
En guise de tête de lit, habiller le mur d'un revêtement en cuir : cela permet d'éviter les structures encombrantes.
Wenn man anstelle des Kopfteils eines Bettes eine Fellverkleidung an der Wand anbringt, kann man auf klobige Strukturen verzichten.

396 Fold-away beds that are hidden in a built-in closet are ideal when a bedroom doubles as a work space.
Les lits convertibles qui disparaissent dans une armoire encastrée sont idéals lorsque la pièce fait également office de bureau.
Klappbetten, die man in einem Schrank verbirgt, eignen sich ausgezeichnet für Bereiche, die auch als Arbeitsräume dienen.

397 Bunk beds help solve problems of space in children's bedrooms.
Les lits superposés sont la solution idéale aux problèmes d'espace dans les chambres d'enfants.
Etagenbetten lösen das Platzproblem in Kinderzimmern.

398 A headboard in the form of a single long shelf is a substitute for a bedside table.

Les têtes de lit, sous forme de grande étagère, remplacent les tables de chevet.
Kopfteile in Form eines einzigen, langen Regals ersetzen Nachttische.

399 Lift beds are a little cramped but they have the advantage of great storage capacity.
Avec les canapés convertibles le lit est plus compact, et la capacité de rangement plus importante.
Klappbare Kanapees sind kompakter als Betten, bieten aber viel Lagerraum.

400 Smooth, pale-colored blankets and bedcovers make a bed less obtrusive and help it to blend in with the rest of the room.
Les édredons et couvertures unis et de couleurs claires allègent visuellement le lit et l'intègrent au reste de l'espace.
Glatte Federbetten und Decken in hellen Farben lassen das Bett leichter wirken und lassen es mit der Umgebung verschmelzen.

© Jordi Miralle

© Shania Shegedyn

© Stefan Meye

© Trevor Main

401 Low, wide stools can serve as both seats and side tables.
Les tabourets larges et bas peuvent servir de sièges ou de tables d'appoint.
Breite, niedrige Hocker dienen als Sitze oder Beistelltische.

402 Bedside tables do not have to follow a single pattern; asymmetrical features make it possible to choose furniture that fits into the space available.
Les tables de chevet ne sont pas obligées d'être identiques : les asymétries permettent de choisir des meubles en accord avec l'espace disponible.
Nachttische müssen nicht immer gleich sein. Wenn sie nicht symmetrisch sind, kann man die Möbel dem zur Verfügung stehenden Platz entsprechend wählen.

403 It is advisable to opt for low chests of drawers to avoid diminishing the sense of spaciousness.
Opter de préférence pour des commodes et des placards bas ou de faible hauteur, permet de ne pas entraver la sensation d'espace.
Damit der Raum nicht optisch verkleinert wird, sollten Kommoden und Schubladenschränke nicht zu hoch sein.

404 Table units on rollers can serve for reading or enjoying breakfast in bed and, during the day, for storing blankets at the foot of the bed.

© Stefan Meyer

Les tables consoles sur roulettes servent pour lire ou pour prendre le petit déjeuner au lit. Dans la journée, placées au pied du lit, elles accueillent les couvertures.
Konsolentische mit Rädern dienen zum Lesen und zum Frühstücken im Bett. Tagsüber kann man sie neben das Bett stellen und die Decken darauf legen.

5 Poufs adjust very easily to any corner of a room and are particularly useful when only one couch can fit into a sitting room.
Les poufs qui se posent n'importe où, sont une solution idéale lorsque le salon ne peut accueillir qu'un seul divan.
Puffs passen in jede Ecke und sind eine praktische Lösung, wenn kein Platz für ein Sofa vorhanden ist.

6 Large storage chests can be turned into a seat if a cushion is placed on top.
Avec un coussin posé dessus, les grands coffres de rangement se transforment en siège.
Truhen zum Aufbewahren von Objekten werden mit einem Kissen zu einem Sitzplatz.

7 Glass cabinets fixed to a wall keep the floor uncluttered and make a room look bigger.
Les vitrines murales dégagent le sol et de ce fait, agrandissent les espaces de vie.

Vitrinen an der Wand halten den Boden frei, und lassen so den Raum größer wirken.

408 Metal baskets are ideal for storing food in a kitchen.
Les structures dotées de paniers en métal sont parfaites pour stocker les aliments dans la cuisine.
Strukturen aus Metallkörben eignen sich ausgezeichnet zum Aufbewahren von Lebensmitteln in der Küche.

409 If a dining room is very small, a narrow dresser can be set in a corridor, under a mirror or picture.
Si la salle à manger est très petite, placer les buffets étroits dans le couloir, sous un miroir ou un tableau.
Wenn das Esszimmer klein ist, kann man eine kleine Anrichte unter einen Spiegel oder ein Bild in den Flur stellen.

410 Wall racks for magazines help keep a room tidy and take up a minimal amount of space.
Les porte-revues muraux, outil de rangement très utile, occupent un espace minime.
Zeitungshalter an der Wand helfen beim Ordnung halten und nehmen nur sehr wenig Platz weg.

411 Trestles supporting worktops can be used to hold shelves, allowing essential items to be kept tidily whilst still being close at hand.
On peut installer des étagères entre les tréteaux qui soutiennent les plans de travail pour avoir sous la main, et bien rangés, les objets les plus utiles.
Böcke, die Arbeitstische halten, nehmen Regale auf. So hat man die notwendigen Objekte stets zur Hand und gut geordnet.

412 If an office doubles as another setting, a chest of drawers with a folding table top can be transformed into a desk.
Si le bureau est intégré dans une pièce de la maison, s'équiper de préférence de secrétaires ou de commodes à rabat pliable qui se transforme en écritoire.
Wenn das Büro einen Bereich in einem anderen Raum einnimmt, eignet sich Sekretäre oder Kommoden mit klappbaren Tischen, die zu einem Schreibtisch werden.

413 An office can be set up in any room with just one table barely bigger than a laptop on a central support, complemented by a shelf unit on rollers.
Avec une table dotée d'un pilier central, d'un plan de travail à peine plus grand que l'ordinateur portable et d'une bibliothèque basse sur roulettes, on peut transporter son bureau d'un coin à l'autre de la pièce.
Ein Büro, das aus einem Tisch mit einem zentralen Fuß, einer Tischplatte, die kaum größer als das Laptop ist und einem niedrigen Bücherschrank mit Rädern besteht, kann in jeden Raum verlagert werden.

© Gogortza & Llorell

The same high bookcase that separates a work area from the rest of the home can act as the support for a table with a wide top.

L'étagère qui sert de cloison de séparation entre la zone de travail et le reste de la maison peut servir de support à un large plan de travail.

Das gleiche hohe Regal, das den Arbeitsbereich von den übrigen Räumen abtrennt, dient als Halterung für den Tisch mit der breiten Platte.

Chests with a cushion on top can serve as a seat for a desk and also be used to store files and documents.

Les grands coffres dotés d'un coussin permettent de s'asseoir face au bureau et d'y ranger documents et papiers.

Gegenüber des Schreibtischs befinden sich Truhen mit Kissen, auf die man sich setzen und in denen man Aktenordner und Papiere aufbewahren kann.

When a work area is set in an open space or passageway, computer tables with a metal grille will blend into the surroundings.

Lorsque le coin bureau est dans un lieu ouvert ou de passage, les tables d'ordinateurs à résille métallique se fondent à l'espace.

Wenn sich der Arbeitsbereich in einem offenen Raum oder einem Durchgangsraum befindet, verschmelzen Tische aus Metallgitter mit der Umgebung.

Movable shelves fixed to a vertical metal rail can be used to keep a fax machine, a printer, card indexes and other essential items.

Les étagères pivotantes, le long d'un rail métallique vertical, peuvent soutenir le fax, l'imprimante, les fichiers et tous les instruments nécessaires sous forme de colonne.

Regale, die sich um eine vertikale Metallschiene drehen, bieten Platz für das Fax, den Drucker, die Karteikästen und alle anderen notwendigen Objekte.

418 A narrow closet with adjustable folding shelves can be turned into a desk complete with a bookcase; the whole unit disappears as soon as the closet is shut.

Une armoire étroite à planches réglables peut se transformer en bureau avec des étagères. Elle disparaît dés que les portes du meuble sont fermées.

Ein schmaler Schrank mit verschiebbaren und klappbaren Regalbrettern kann zu einem Schreibtisch mit Regal werden, der verschwindet, wenn man die Türen dieses Möbelstücks schließt.

419 In very narrow rooms, L-shape desks help gain work space.

Dans les pièces très étroites, les bureaux en L offrent un gain d'espace.

In schmalen Zimmern gewinnt man durch L-förmige Schreibtische Raum.

420 Shoe holders are narrow and therefore perfectly suited to storing papers without taking up much space.

Les meubles de cordonnier sont étroits et donc idéals pour ranger des papiers sans prendre trop de place.

Schuhschränke sind sehr schmal und eignen sich deshalb gut zum Aufbewahren von Papieren, ohne viel Platz einzunehmen.

© Joan Mundó

© Alejandro Bahamó

© Alejandro Bahamó

© Rupert Steiner

© John Gollings

© Ake Eson Lindmann

© Leven Betts Stud

© Bjorg Arnasdottir

421 Even the smallest of bathrooms need not forsake a bathtub. Oval tubs occupy less space than the traditional models.
Une salle de bains, aussi petite soit-elle, ne doit pas pour autant se priver de baignoire. A cet effet, privilégier la forme ovale, moins encombrante que la forme traditionnelle.
Egal, wie klein ein Bad ist, man muss auf die Badewanne nicht verzichten. Ovale Badewannen benötigen weniger Platz als die in traditioneller Form.

422 Shower drapes with pockets obviate the need for shelves.
Les rideaux de douche dotés de poches de rangement remplacent les étagères.
Duschvorhänge mit Taschen dienen als Regale.

423 Mirrors must be large, to allow them to reflect as much light as possible.
Les miroirs doivent être très grands pour refléter un maximum de lumière.
Die Spiegel sollten groß sein, damit sie soviel Licht wie möglich reflektieren.

424 Round washbasins and toilets make it easier to move around in a smal bathroom.
Les lavabos, les bidets et les cabinets arrondis facilitent la circulation dans les salles de bains de taille réduite.

© Nuria Fuentes

Wenn Waschbecken und Toiletten runde Formen haben, kann man sich einfacher in kleinen Bädern bewegen.

Transparent glass screens leave the wall of the shower visible and thus enhance the sense of spaciousness.
Les pare-douche en verre transparent laissent voir le mur de la douche et agrandissent ainsi l'espace.
Glastüren aus transparentem Glas lassen die Wand der Dusche sichtbar und vergrößern so scheinbar den Raum.

Bidets are an option for very small bathrooms only capable of holding basic equipment.
Les bidets inodores sont une solution pour les salles de bains très petites qui ne peuvent accueillir que le mobilier de base.
Bidet-Toiletten sind eine Lösung für sehr kleine Bäder, in denen nur die grundlegendsten Elemente Platz haben.

Furniture can only be put in the space underneath the washbasin if the latter is fixed to the wall, without any support rising from the floor.
Les meubles qui se rangent sous l'évier sont peu avantageux en termes d'espace, sauf s'ils sont suspendus et n'atteignent pas le sol.
Einbauschränke unter dem Waschbecken sind nicht sehr vorteilhaft in kleinen Räumen, es sei denn, sie hängen an der Wand und reichen nicht bis zum Boden.

428 Aluminum shelves go well with all types of bathrooms and help give an impression of spaciousness.
Les étagères d'aluminium se marient à tous les styles de salle de bains et permettent de les agrandir.
Aluminiumregale passen gut in alle Badezimmer und lassen den Raum größer wirken.

429 A wide shelf attached to the wall can serve as a bench, and baskets or metal boxes can be stored underneath it.
Une large planche encastrée dans le mur sert de banc, sous lequel il est possible d'entreposer paniers et boîtes de rangement en métal.
Ein breites Brett an der Wand dient als Bank, unter die man Körbe oder Metallkisten zum Aufbewahren von Objekten stellen kann.

430 Round aluminum washbasins set in a glass top are less obtrusive than traditional ceramic sinks.
Les vasques rondes en aluminium posées sur un plan de toilette de verre sont moins encombrantes que les traditionnelles en céramique.
Runde Aluminiumwaschbecken über einer Ablage aus Glas wirken leichter als traditionelle Waschbecken aus Keramik.

© Nuria Fuentes

rohibido estacionar. Grac

© Alejandro Baham

431 Modules with separate sections for the stove, sink and worktops allow kitchen to be installed in any part of a home.

Les modules qui accueillent séparément les unités de cuisson, le lave-vaisselle et les plans de travail pour la préparation des aliments permettent d'installer la cuisine dans n'importe quel coin de la maison

Module, in denen der Herd, das Spülbecken und die Arbeitsplatten getrennt voneinander untergebracht sind, ermöglichen es, Küchen in jedem Raum des Hauses zu installieren.

432 Closets with transparent doors seem to take up less space than those with opaque doors.

Les armoires aux portes transparentes maximalisent l'espace plus que les portes opaques.

Schränke mit transparenten Türen lassen den Raum weiter wirken als undurchsichtige Türen.

433 Electrical equipment like the oven, microwave, dishwasher and coffee machine can be kept on a single vertical axis by means of strategically placed shelves.

L'électroménager comme le four traditionnel, le four à micro-ondes, le lave-vaisselle et la cafetière peuvent s'installer dans un même élémen en colonne grâce à un système d'étagères adéquat.

Küchengeräte wie Herde, Mikrowellenherde, Geschirrspüler und Kaffeemaschinen können mit geeigneten Regalen im selben Turm untergebracht werden.

© Luuk Kramer

© Yael Pincus

Round units with rollers are ideal for square kitchens.

Les îlots arrondis, sur roulettes, sont idéals pour les cuisines très carrées.

Runde Inseln mit Rädern eignen sich ausgezeichnet für quadratische Küchen.

Mini-kitchens containing a small refrigerator, a sink, hot plates, drawers, a worktop, an extractable table and storage facilities are appropriate for single-space houses.

Les mini cuisines que intègrent en un monobloc le mini réfrigérateur, le lave-vaisselle, les plaques, les tiroirs, le plan de travail, une table escamotable et des espaces de rangement sont parfaites pour les espaces de vie unique.

Miniküchen, bei denen in einem Karren ein Minikühlschrank, die Spüle, die Kochplatten, die Schubladen, die Arbeitsfläche, ein ausziehbarer Tisch und Schränke untergebracht sind, eignen sich für Wohnungen mit nur einem Raum.

Utensils that do not fit in closets can be hung from a long metal bar fixed underneath them.

Une barre de métal installée sous les placards du haut permet de suspendre les ustensiles qui ne rentrent pas dans les armoires.

An einer langen Metallstange unter den Schränken kann man die Küchenutensilien aufhängen, die nicht in die Schränke passen.

Mesh baskets and hooks inside closet doors are other space-saving devices.

Les paniers à résilles et crochets, fixés à l'intérieur des portes des armoires, sont un gain d'espace.

Körbe mit Gittern und Haken im Inneren der Küchentüren helfen Platz zu sparen.

438 High-capacity extractor hoods can be set on a wall and take up little space.

Les hottes d'aspiration intense s'installent sur le mur et occupent une surface limitée.

Abzugshauben mit besonders hoher Leistung werden an der Wand angebracht und nehmen so nur eine kleine Fläche ein.

439 In single-space homes, long kitchen units not only separate the kitchen from the living room but also serve as an eating area.

Dans les maisons à espace de vie unique, les îlots en longueur séparent la cuisine du salon et servent de salle à manger.

In Wohnungen mit nur einem einzigen Raum trennen längliche Kücheninseln die Küche vom Wohnzimmer und dienen gleichzeitig als Esstisch.

440 Corner modules acquire additional storing capacity when fitted with movable trays.

Les modules d'angle offrent une grande capacité de rangement grâce aux étagères à tourniquet.

Wenn man Eckschränke mit drehbaren Regalen versieht, passt noch viel mehr rein.

441   Drawers can be inserted into staircases leading up to high beds.
Les tiroirs en forme d'escalier permettent également d'accéder aux l
superposés.
Treppenförmige Schubladenschränke dienen auch zum Aufstieg zu d
Hochbetten.

442   Inflatable furniture is comfortable, fun and easy to move around.
Les meubles gonflables sont pratiques, amusants pour les enfants et
faciles à ranger.
Aufblasbare Möbel sind bequem, die Kinder finden sie lustig und mar
kann sie einfach verstauen.

443   Large plastic or wooden boxes can be packed with toys and also dou
as seats.
Les grandes boîtes en plastique ou bois, pour ranger les jouets, serve
aussi de siège.
Große Kisten aus Kunststoff oder Holz, in denen man die Spielzeuge
verstauen kann, dienen als Sitz.

444   Beds can be fitted with a big drawer underneath the mattress; this is
ideal for storing bulky objects.
Les lits gigognes ont un grand tiroir sous le matelas, idéal pour range
les objets encombrants.
Das Bett hat eine große Schublade unter der Matratze, in der man gr
Objekte unterbringen kann.

© Jordi Sarrà

© Jordi Sar

Rounded corners on tables blunt the impact of any knocks suffered by children while playing.

Les tables de jeu, aux angles arrondis, évitent aux enfants de se blesser.

Durch abgerundete Ecken an den Spieltischen wird vermieden, dass sich die Kinder beim Spielen an den Ecken wehtun.

Bookcases designed to receive additional modules can be adapted to children's changing needs with the passing of the years.

Les étagères auxquelles on peut ajouter des modules s'adaptent aux besoins des enfants au fur et à mesure qu'ils grandissent.

An die Regale können Module angefügt werden. Wenn das Kind älter wird, können sie entsprechend den sich verändernden Bedürfnissen angepasst werden.

Chest of drawers with a slide can bring both order and fun to any part of the house.

Les tiroirs en forme de toboggan conjuguent ordre et jeu dans n'importe quel espace de la maison.

Schubladen, die gleichzeitig als Rutsche dienen, sorgen überall im Haus für Ordnung und man kann damit spielen.

Cribs with removable rails can be used as a bed once a child is no longer a baby.

Les berceaux aux rambardes amovibles servent de lit lorsque le bébé grandit.

Wiegen mit abnehmbaren Geländern werden zu einem normalen Kinderbett, wenn das Kind aus dem Babyalter heraus ist.

449 Baskets allow toys to remain in view in an orderly fashion. They can be hung from a steel bar to occupy less space.

Les paniers permettent que les jouets soient visibles et rangés. Pour qu'ils occupent peu d'espace, les accrocher le long d'une barre d'acier.

In den Körben kann man die Spielzeuge gut geordnet und sichtbar aufbewahren. Damit sie weniger Platz wegnehmen, hängen sie an einer Stahlstange.

450 A clothes rack with a shelf can serve for storing storybooks and hanging clothes or accessories.

Les portemanteaux à étagères servent à ranger des livres de contes et à suspendre les vêtements ou les accessoires.

Kleiderständer mit Regalen dienen zum Aufbewahren der Märchenbücher und zum Aufhängen von Kleidern und Zubehör.

© Jordi Sarrà

© Murray Fredericks

451 Teak furniture is particularly suited to outdoor use as it stands up we to inclement weather.

Le bois de teck est un des meilleurs bois d'extérieur. Les meubles de cette matière résistent bien au mauvais temps et aux intempéries.

Teakholz eignet sich ausgezeichnet für draußen. Möbel aus diesem Material sind sehr wetterfest.

452 Wooden platforms can stand on the ground, without any need for construction work, to give an impression of spaciousness. They are superbly set off by steel furniture.

Les cloisons de bois se posent facilement sur le carrelage et accentu la sensation d'espace. Privilégier alors les meubles en acier pour introduire un contraste.

Für ein Podium aus Holz sind keine Bauarbeiten notwendig. Es kann dem Boden aufgestellt und verleiht dem Raum mehr Größe. I diesem Fall entsteht durch Stahlmöbel ein Kontrast.

453 Wood or metal chests can be used to keep gardening tools and also double as a seat.

Les grands coffres de bois ou métal permettent de ranger les outils de jardinage, tout en servant de sièges.

In Truhen aus Holz oder Metall kann man Gartenutensilien aufbewahr und sie dienen gleichzeitig als Sitz.

454 Double-flap gate-leg tables take up very little space when they are folded up and they can be kept indoors when it rains.

© Shania Sheged

Les tables pliables à deux battants prennent peu d'espace. En cas de pluie, une fois pliées, on peut les ranger à l'intérieur de la maison.

Klapptische mit zwei Flügeln nehmen sehr wenig Raum ein, wenn sie zusammengeklappt sind, und sie können bei Regen im Haus aufbewahrt werden.

5 Stone benches running along a wall help take full advantage of the available space and create different settings within a terrace.

Les bancs de pierre ou bordures qui filent le long du mur permettent d'optimiser l'espace et de créer des petits coins sympathiques sur la terrasse.

Durch Bänke aus Holz oder Stein an der Wand wird der Platz maximal genutzt und man kann verschiedene Bereiche auf der Terrasse schaffen.

6 Flat awnings supported by thin posts at one end do not encroach on the space when they are fully extended.

Les toiles planes fixées aux extrémités sur de fins piliers ne réduisent pas l'espace lorsqu'elles sont tendues au maximum.

Flache Sonnendächer stehen an ihren Enden auf feinen Säulen, die den Raum nicht kleiner wirken lassen, selbst wenn die gesamte Terrasse überdacht ist.

7 A row of potted shrubs guarantees privacy from the neighbors.

Une rangée de grands pots de plantes dans le style d'arbustes, préserve l'intimité et protège des voisins.

Große, aneinander gereihte Blumentöpfen mit Büschen schirmen gegen die Blicke der Nachbarn ab.

458 Folding hammocks are unobtrusive and can be stored easily when not in use.

Les hamacs pliables n'obstruent pas la vue et, inutilisés, sont faciles à ranger.

Zusammenklappbare Liegestühle wirken leicht und können einfach verstaut werden.

459 Square cushions can be used like small mattresses; they are very decorative, practical and easy to stack.

Les coussins carrés semblables à des oreillers sont très décoratifs, pratiques et facilement empilables.

Quadratische Kissen, die Matratzen ähneln, sind sehr dekorativ, praktisch und einfach zu stapeln.

460 Seats made with synthetic fibers have a delicate appearance and are available in bright colors.

Les sièges en fibre synthétique sont légers et riches en couleurs gaies.

Stühle aus Synthetikfaser wirken leicht und es gibt sie in kräftigen Farben.

© Nuria Fuentes

© Gogortza & Llorella

© Jordi Miralle

© Shania Shegedyn

461 Large pictures standing on the floor help make walls look bigger.
Les grands tableaux appuyés sur le sol permettent d'agrandir les murs
Große Bilder, die auf dem Boden stehen, lassen die Wände weit wirken

462 Contrary to popular belief, the bigger the mirror, the greater the subsequent sense of spaciousness.
Contrairement aux idées reçues, plus les miroirs occupent de la place, plus la sensation d'espace est importante.
Auch wenn man das Gegenteil annehmen könnte, lassen Spiegel den Raum weiter wirken, je mehr Fläche sie einnehmen.

463 A scattering of pictures makes a wall look smaller. It is advisable to group them together to leave as much space uncovered as possible.
Les tableaux dispersés réduisent visuellement les murs. Il convient de les regrouper dans le même coin pour libérer la plus grande partie de la surface.
Zerstreut aufgehängte Bilder reduzieren die Fläche visuell. Es ist besser sie in einer Zone zusammen aufzuhängen und den größten Teil der Wand frei zu lassen.

464 An accumulation of objects in a small room makes it look cramped. A carefully lit picture is sufficient to give a space personality.
L'accumulation d'objets dans les pièces réduites les rapetisse encore plus. Un tableau bien éclairé suffit pour donner du caractère à l'espace de vie.

© Margherita Spiluttini

© Nuria Fuentes

Durch die Anhäufung von Objekten in einem kleinen Raum wirkt dieser noch kleiner. Ein Bild mit einer guten Beleuchtung reicht aus, um einem Raum Persönlichkeit zu verleihen.

5 Pictures with abstract images and large blocks of color help create an impression of spaciousness.
Les peintures abstraites et les tableaux dotés d'une grande surface colorée agrandissent l'espace.
Abstrakte Gemälde mit großen Farbflächen lassen den Raum ebenfalls größer wirken.

56 If there is no space for a free-standing mirror in a bedroom, one can be fixed inside the doors of a closet.
Si la chambre à coucher est trop petite pour y placer un miroir sur pied, en installer un sur la face interne des portes de l'armoire.
Wenn das Schlafzimmer für einen Spiegel bis zum Boden zu klein ist, kann dieser in den Türen des Schrankes angebracht werden.

57 A large mirror set in front of a sitting-room window helps reflect sunlight throughout a room.
Un grand miroir face à la fenêtre du salon permet d'irradier la lumière naturelle dans toute la pièce.
Ein großer Spiegel, der gegenüber vom Wohnzimmerfenster hängt, reflektiert Tageslicht in den gesamten Raum.

468 Smooth metal frames are less eye-catching than wooden models and add a modern touch.
Les cadres de métal lisse sont visuellement plus légers que ceux en bois et apportent une touche de modernité.
Rahmen aus glattem Metall wirken visuell leichter und moderner als Holzrahmen.

469 Baroque-style mirror frames are only appropriate for small spaces if they are the sole element on a wall.
Les cadres baroques pour les miroirs ne sont valables que dans les petits espaces, à condition d'être le seul élément de décor sur les murs.
Spiegelrahmen im Barockstil sollten in kleinen Räumen nur aufgehängt werden, wenn weiter nichts an der Wand hängt.

470 A screen can be turned into a display area for portraits.
Un paravent peut se transformer en un support pour exposer des photos.
Der Wandschirm kann zu einem großen Fotorahmen werden.

© Artcoust

© Artcoustic

© John Gollings

© Luis Hevia

471 Any white wall can be used to project images from a television, DVD player or computer, thus enabling this equipment to be tucked out of sight.

Tout mur blanc est idéal pour projeter des images de la télévision, du DVD ou de l'ordinateur, on évite ainsi la présence de n'importe quel écran.

Jede weiße Fläche an einer Wand eignet sich dafür, Bilder vom Fernseher, DVD-Player oder Computer darauf zu projizieren, so dass man diese Geräte verbergen kann.

472 A sitting room's electrical equipment can all be concentrated into a single area on shelves attached to a vertical axis.

Les appareils électriques du salon peuvent être réunis dans le même coin, posés sur des socles en forme de colonne.

Die Geräte im Wohnzimmer können in einem einzigen Bereich auf Regalbrettern verstaut werden, so dass ein Turm entsteht.

473 A television should be set at a low height in order to avoid taking up too much wall space. Corner benches allow it to be placed in any part of the room.

Il est préférable d'installer la télévision à faible hauteur pour réduire l'espace occupé sur le mur. Les bancs d'angle permettent de la placer dans n'importe quel coin.

Der Fernseher sollte niedrig stehen, damit er nicht zuviel Raum an der Wand einnimmt. Eckbänke kann man in jeder Ecke aufstellen.

© Luuk Kramer

4   Loudspeakers are more stylish when they are mounted on aluminum stands; the sound quality is also improved when they are raised from the floor.
Les hauts-parleurs montés sur des socles d'aluminium sont très stylés. De plus, la qualité du son n'en est que meilleure.
Die Lautsprecher wirken edler, wenn sie auf einem Ständer aus Aluminium stehen. Dies verbessert auch die Tonqualität.

5   In very small spaces, a gap in a bookcase can be used to hold audio and video equipment.
Dans les espaces réduits, installer de préférence appareils audio et vidéo sur une étagère vide.
In sehr kleinen Räumen sollte man ein Regal für die Audio- und Videogeräte benutzen.

6   Wall supports for electrical equipment help to keep a floor uncluttered.
Les supports muraux permettent de libérer le sol.
Durch Wandhalterungen bleibt der Boden frei.

7   Wireless music systems can be set up in any available space and eliminate the nuisance of cables.
Les chaînes de musique *sans fil* peuvent occuper n'importe quel vide disponible et libèrent l'espace de câbles qui entravent la circulation.
Musikanlagen mit Wireless-System können überall aufgestellt werden, weil keine störenden Kabel den Durchgang behindern.

478   In small kitchens, it is advisable to opt for units that group together the extractor hood, glass stove top, oven and dishwater on the same vertical plane.
Dans les petites cuisines, préférer le choix d'équipements qui regroupent la hotte, la plaque vitrocéramique, le four et le lave-vaisselle sur un même plan vertical.
In kleinen Küchen sollte man sich für Mobiliar entscheiden, bei dem die Dunstabzugshaube, die Glaskeramikplatte, der Backofen und die Spülmaschine in dem gleichen, vertikalen Modul untergebracht sind.

479   A closet in a corridor or near the kitchen can be used to store the washing machine, dryer and ironing board.
Une armoire dans le couloir ou près de la cuisine peut accueillir le lave-linge, le sèche-linge et la table à repasser.
Ein Schrank im Flur oder in Küchennähe kann die Waschmaschine, den Trockner und das Bügelbrett aufnehmen.

480   Open spaces in plasterboard walls serve as shelves that can unobtrusively hold audio and video equipment.
Les niches ou alcôves ouvertes dans les murs maçonnés servent d'étagères où déposer les appareils audio et vidéo, sans gêner la vue.
Öffnungen in Pladurwänden dienen als Regale, auf denen man die Audio- und Videogeräte aufstellen kann, ohne dass sie visuell stören.

© Artcoustic

© Reto Guntli/Zapaimage

© Reto Guntli/Zapaimages

481 The accumulation of small objects counteracts any sense of spaciousness, so it is advisable to confine yourself to a few large ornaments that can highlight specific parts of a home.

L'accumulation de petits objets n'agrandit pas l'espace : mieux vaut en avoir peu et de plus grande taille pour séparer certaines zones de la maison.

Viele kleine Objekte lassen auch den Raum kleiner wirken. Es ist besser wenige größere Objekte zu haben, um einzelne Bereiche in der Wohnung voneinander zu unterscheiden.

482 Cushions must be used in moderation as a decorative element because they can clutter up a setting.

Les coussins en tant qu'éléments décoratifs sont à utiliser avec modération, car ils réduisent l'espace.

Kissen als Dekorationsobjekte sollten zurückhaltend benutzt werden, weil sie viel Platz benötigen.

483 Blankets are effective for creating contrasts with furniture because they do not take up any space, as well as having the benefit of being functional.

Les couvertures permettent de créer des jeux de contrastes avec les meubles : elles ne prennent pas de place et sont fonctionnelles.

Mit Decken kann man Kontraste zu den Möbeln schaffen, weil sie kaum Platz brauchen und funktionell sind.

© Giovanna Piemonti

4   Colored glass vases are more appropriate than opaque ones in small
    corners, as they allow light to pass through them.
    Dans les petits coins, les carafes de verre coloré sont plus appropriées
    que les opaques, car elles laissent passer la lumière.
    Farbige Kristallkrüge eignen sich in kleinen Ecken besser als
    undurchsichtige Krüge, weil sie Licht durchlassen.

5   Kitchen closets with room for a plate rack on the shelf above the sink
    are a good space-saving device.
    Les armoires de cuisine qui permettent d'installer un égouttoir sur
    l'étagère au-dessus de l'évier sont un gain d'espace.
    In den Küchenschränken befindet sich eine Abtropfvorrichtung auf dem
    Regal über der Spüle, um Platz zu sparen.

6   In order to maintain the order that is so essential to a small space,
    baskets made of natural fiber can be used to store magazines.
    Pour favoriser l'ordre dans un petit espace, les paniers de fibre naturelle
    peuvent servir de porte-revues.
    Um die notwendige Ordnung in kleinen Räumen zu wahren, dienen die
    Körbe aus Naturfasern als Zeitungsständer.

7   Glass candelabras are ideal for setting up interplays of contrasting light
    in rustic settings.
    Les chandeliers de verre sont parfaits pour créer des jeux de contraste
    dans les atmosphères rustiques.

Kandelaber aus Glas dienen als Kontrast in rustikal dekorierten
Wohnungen.

488   Boxes covered with leather or decorative paper can be stacked to
      imitate a chest of drawers or set in a line to store small objects.
      Les boîtes habillées de cuir ou de papiers décoratifs peuvent s'empiler
      pour former une grande boîte ou être placées sur une étagère pour y
      ranger des petits objets.
      Die mit Leder oder Tapeten verkleideten Kisten können zu einem
      Schubladenschrank gestapelt oder auf einem Regal in einer Reihe
      aufgestellt werden, um kleine Objekte aufzubewahren.

489   Pottery vases in various sizes can be arranged along a shelf close to the
      ceiling to cut off very high walls.
      Les cruches en céramique de différentes formes, disposées sur une
      étagère près du plafond, permettent de diminuer visuellement la
      hauteur de murs très hauts.
      Keramikkrüge in verschiedenen Formen auf dem Regal in Deckennähe
      lassen sehr hohe Wände niedriger wirken.

490   A rustic painter's ladder leaning against a wall can provide an original
      support on which to hang magazines or blankets.
      Un escalier de peinture en bois rustique, appuyé contre le mur, est une
      idée originale pour accrocher des revues ou draper des couvertures.
      Eine an die Wand gestützte Malerleiter aus rustikalem Holz ist eine
      originelle Lösung zum Aufhängen von Zeitungen und Decken.

© Mark York / Red Cover

© Jordi Miral

© Henry Wilson / Red Cover

491 The most efficient means of heating a house is under-floor heating, as this distributes heat uniformly.

Dans une maison, le chauffage par le sol est la méthode la plus efficace, car il distribue la chaleur de manière uniforme.

Der beste Heizungstyp für eine Wohnung ist eine Fußbodenheizung, weil sie die Wärme gleichmäßig verteilt.

492 Extremely thin air-conditioning systems for hot/cold regulations occu the same space as an average picture and offer the same features as traditional models.

Les climatiseurs et radiateurs extra plats prennent la place d'un table moyen et sont aussi performants que les traditionnels.

Extraflache Heizkörper nehmen nur so viel Platz wie ein mittelgroßes Bild ein und sind genauso leistungsstark wie die traditionellen Heizungen.

493 Electric fireplaces are flat, compact and as capable of creating the same cozy atmosphere as the real things.

Les cheminées électriques sont plates et compactes et donnent la même impression de foyer que les traditionnelles.

Elektrische Kamine sind flach und kompakt und strahlen die gleiche Wärme wie Holzkamine aus.

494 Very thin radiators that adapt to the form and color of a wall enhance the sense of spaciousness.

© Matteo Piazza

© Matteo Piazza

Les radiateurs extra plats adaptés à la forme et couleur du mur agrandissent l'espace.
Extraflache Heizkörper, die in ihrer Form und Farbe an die Wand angepasst sind, lassen den Raum größer wirken.

495 The space occupied by heating equipment in a bathroom can be exploited by installing radiators in the form of a bench.
Les radiateurs en forme de banc sont une autre façon d'utiliser judicieusement l'espace occupé par les éléments de chauffage dans une salle de bains.
Im Bad kann man den Platz, den die Heizkörper einnehmen, nutzen, indem man Elemente in Form einer Bank verwendet.

496 Latest hot-air heating systems are designed as a step that fits underneath a window.
Les nouveaux appareils d'air chaud se présentent sous forme de gradins à installer sous les baies vitrées.
Neuen Heißluftheizungen haben die Form eines Absatzes, den man unter Fenstern anbringen kann.

497 Gas fireplaces are attached to the wall like a screen. Models with a metal frame go well with settings dominated by stone.
Les cheminées à gaz se découpent sur le mur comme un écran. Celles qui disposent d'un cadre métallique se marient bien dans les espaces de vie dominés par la pierre.

Gaskamine hängen wie ein Bildschirm an der Wand. Modelle mit Metallrahmen passen gut in Wohnungen, in denen es viel Naturstein gibt.

498 It is a good idea to install a tubular panel with a hanger in a bathroom, not only to keep the area warm but also to dry towels.
Dans les salles de bains, pour plus de commodité, installer un panneau tubulaire pour accrocher les serviettes et les sécher tout en réchauffant l'atmosphère.
In Bädern sollte man ein Heizkörperelement installieren, das gleichzeitig als Handtuchtrockner dient.

499 Radiators in the form of thin decorative panels can also be used to divide a space.
Les radiateurs en forme de minces panneaux décoratifs permettent également de diviser les espaces de vie.
Heizkörper in Form von dekorativen Paneelen können gleichzeitig als Raumteiler dienen.

500 The modern designs for metal fireplaces take up very little space and can be hung from the ceiling.
Les cheminées métalliques, au design contemporain et peu encombrantes, peuvent être suspendues au plafond.
Metallkamine in zeitgemäßem Design nehmen wenig Platz weg und können an der Decke aufgehängt werden.

Special thanks to Remerciements particuliers à Mit besonderem Dank an

1100 Architect
4Site
Adhoc MSL
Andrew Berman Architect
Architectuurcentrale Thijs Asselbergs
Artcoustic
Bauart
BBP Architects
BEHF Architekten
Bent Architecture
Beriot, Bernardini & Gorini
Bisazza
B. Lux
Casadesús
Cassandra Komplex
Claesson Koivisto Rune Architects
Cristina Rodríguez
Daniele di Monte
Ellen Rapelius, Xavier Franquesa
Eric Rosen Architects
Espinet-Ubach Arquitectes i Associats
Extratapete
Felipe Assadi
Flavia Cancian, Renata Furlanetto
GCA Arquitectes Associats
Gnosis Architettura
Groep Delta Architectuur
Hayball Leonard Stent, Sue Carr

Hobby A.
Itzai Paritzki, Paola Liani
Ivan Kroupa Architects
Jaime Sanahuja, Emilio Cubillos, José M.ª Medrano
Javier Hernández Mingo
Javier Iriondo Silvan
Johnson Chu
Josep M. Font/Greek
Leven Betts Studio
LG Electronics
Luigi Colani
Marble Fairbanks Architects
Marc Rabiner
Michael Haberz
Nik Karalis
Peter Ebner, Franziska Ullmann
Peter Tyberghyen
Raumteam 92
RCR Arquitectes
Satoshi Okada Architects
Stone Design
Studio Roberto Mascazzini
Tang Kawasaki Studio
Tapeten Agentur
Tatanka Ideenvertriebsgesellschaft
Tres Tintas BCN
Veruso
Whitcher Matyear Architects